My Memoirs

Volume 1

MY MEMOIRS

Volume 1: 1934 to 1955

AUDREY CLEGG

T

Troubador Publishing Ltd
Unit E2 Airfield Business Park
Harrison Road, Market Harborough
Leicestershire LE16 7UL
Tel: 0116 279 2299
Email: books@troubador.co.uk
Web: www.troubador.co.uk

ISBN 978 1 80514 495 3

British Library Cataloguing in Publication Data.
A catalogue record for this book is available from the British Library.

Typeset in 11pt Minion Pro by Troubador Publishing Ltd, Leicester, UK

I dedicate this to my mother, Nora Jane. Without her love and guidance and her sacrifice, none of this would have been possible.

I also dedicate this to my husband, Derek, for his love, his patience, his wisdom, and the joy he brought into my life.

I must also dedicate it to the two people who made my life complete and gave me a reason to start writing these memoirs. My sons, John and Tim. Without their love and their constant support and encouragement I would never have got this far.

1

As time passes, and each year goes by at an increasingly faster speed, memories fade, become fainter and more difficult to recall. So perhaps it is time to write down what I remember of my childhood.

My earliest memories are of a house in Darlington which I now know to be number 19 Parkside. I must have been about three years old. I remember it being a happy place, though I was then unaware of the circumstances which brought me there. I was to learn of them when I was much older.

To begin at the beginning. When they were married my parents lived in a house in West Hartlepool. I do not have the address. I think the early years of marriage were happy ones if the photographs I have are anything to go by.

I was born in West Hartlepool on Sunday 26th August 1934.

My father was absent. Supposedly away on business at the time. Sadly, it was later discovered that he was having an affair with one of the girls from the office. Those early years must have been very difficult for my mother. She filed for divorce and took me to live in Darlington. She rented number

19 Parkside, and for a while, as far as I was concerned, life was good.

I have no memories of my father other than that of a man who occasionally visited Parkside and cried all the time he was there. The first contact he ever made with me personally was to send me a letter and the gift of a tea set on the occasion of my wedding.

My mother took in two lodgers, my godmother Edna, and her friend Ann. Both were teachers at a local school. As I recall those were happy times for me. It was a nice house with three bedrooms and a bathroom upstairs, quite something in those days!

My bedroom was lovely, I remember it had an alcove which was up two steps and covered with a curtain... a very special place to play with my dolls.

Next door lived Nell and Joe Stephenson with their two children Ann and Eric, both in their teens. Nell took my mother "under her wing" and they remained the very best of friends until the day they died. Also friends for life were Edna and Ann. I think in those early years I was quite spoilt by Nell, Edna and Ann.

Edna came from Middleton-in-Teesdale. She and my mother were friends as young girls. Ann came from Stanhope, and both took me home with them from time to time at weekends.

Obviously the most important person in my life was my wonderful mother – "Mammy" as we said in the north. She was always there, able to solve all problems.

I remember on one occasion I had been playing with a little girl called Agnes – "Nessie" for short. Nessie lived in a house opposite. She was older than me and very bossy. She always refused to let me open the gate. Being prevented from opening a gate seems so trivial now but oh how important it was at the time! On this particular occasion she said that I had told a lie and because of that I would burn in hell. I don't know what the lie was but I remember to this day the terror I felt. I remember my mother consoling me in a warm bath followed by a hot drink and a bedtime hug, and how I felt safe and secure again.

Other memories from that time include an occasion when I had been dressed in a lovely white dress for a special event. I had been told to wait in the living room while my mother finished getting ready. I don't think I was the most obedient child as I was found outside in the coal house with my white dress covered in coal dust! My mother was very angry!

The staircase at number 19 led to the upstairs around the side of the hall in a curve with a banister rail perfect for sliding down. A series of spindles joined the banister to the staircase. For some reason the spaces between the spindles were wider at the top than they were at the bottom. One day I put my head through the banister rail at the top and then knelt down. When I tried to remove my head I was well and truly stuck. I remember screaming blue murder until I was released.

I also remember being confined to bed with measles. I must have been a bad patient because the doctor, a tall stern man called Doctor Woodman, sat by my bed and lectured me about being good. I can't remember exactly what he said but I think it worked!

Doctor Woodman was an excellent doctor. Besides being firm when it was necessary he was also kind, caring and extremely efficient. He cared for me throughout the whole of my childhood and teenage years.

When I was five years old I started school at Dodmire Infants School. I met a girl called Aileen. We used to walk to school together. On the way we passed a shop where they sold 'penny bags'. These bags contained a selection of sweets and small novelties. Each Friday I was given a penny to buy a bag. I still recall the excitement of opening the bag to discover what it contained.

In September 1939, the start of World War Two was to affect our lives greatly. In fact, life would never be the same again for quite some time.

Life was to change for everyone. The owner of Parkside decided to sell the property and as my mother was in no position to buy it we had to find somewhere else to live. This meant that Edna and Ann also had to find alternative accommodation and the loss of their income meant that part-time work was no longer an option for my mother.

After leaving Parkside my mother found work in the canteen of North Road shops, the local railway engine building works.

We went to live with an old woman – a gossip if ever there was one – in a house on Greenbank Road. I started school at Reid Street School.

My first day was quite eventful as I ended up getting lost on the way home. Greenbank Road was a long road probably about half a mile long. The house where I was staying was directly opposite Reid Street, where the school was less than 100 yards' walk. However, a helpful little girl called Jean informed the teacher that she would take me home. She did!!!… to the other end of Greenbank Road by another route. There she left me. Luckily a very kind lady, who found me crying, took me the whole length of Greenbank Road, until I found the right house. After all I was only five years old.

Our stay at this house did not last long. My mother had decided that she would tell me all about my father when she thought I was old enough to understand. I did not miss him as I did not remember him, but our landlady decided to inform me that he was living with another woman in a nearby town. This coupled with the fact that my mother discovered that her private possessions had been searched and things were missing caused her to make a very difficult decision.

2

Until now my mother had managed to make enough money to keep us together. That time was now gone and her only alternative was to ask somebody else for help.

Sadly the only person available was her mother... my grandmother. I say sadly because... well, to explain, I need to tell a little about my mother's life as a child.

My mother was born Nora Jane Harrison on the 4th of June 1909 to Charles and Annie Harrison. She was the seventh child, born when my grandmother was in her forties, and very much unplanned. One child, John, had died soon after childbirth I think. The surviving children were, one girl Matilda, and four boys, Thomas, Charles, Robert and George.

When my mother was very small, her sister Matilda married George. Matilda gave birth to two children, Raymond and Rene. I understand that my mother spent much of her childhood helping her sister with the children.

Sadly, Tilly, as she was called, was in a controlling and abusive marriage. When she was still very young she became ill and eventually died. I don't know the exact circumstances as she died before I was born, and it was never spoken of when I was young. I never knew her, but I remember Raymond and Rene.

Raymond sustained a severe head injury when a slate fell from the roof when he was young. It was suspected that this was the reason for him becoming the black sheep of the family, in other words, it caused a brain injury. I remember being told that he used to disappear for years, then turn up like the proverbial bad penny and then disappear again.

Rene, on the other hand, married Jack. She had two children, a boy named Keith and a girl named Margo. They lived in a bungalow in Barton, a village between Richmond and Darlington. I remember visiting as a child and thinking they must be very, very rich to live in such a beautiful place.

The eldest of my mother's brothers was Tom. It was rumoured that he was my grandmother's favourite, though I still find it hard to understand that anyone can choose a favourite between their children.

I remember my mother telling me about Sally. She said Tom loved her dearly. Sally was Tom's first girlfriend and I do not know exactly what happened but sadly she died at a very young age. Tom eventually met, fell in love with and married a girl called Hilda. I remember Auntie Hilda with great fondness.

Tom fought in the trenches in World War One. He returned home a very sick man, suffering from the effects of gas, and sadly never recovered. My mother recalled lying awake in her bedroom, listening to him fighting for his breath night after night. He and Hilda had a daughter named Margaret and a son named Bert. Sadly Tom did not live to see Bert born. Margaret lives in Gainford in County Durham. Her brother Bert sadly died at his home in Swindon in 2009 or 2010. The brothers, Charles, Robert and George, I remember as my uncles who formed an important part of my childhood.

Charles, known to me as Uncle Charlie, also served in World War One in the trenches. He also came home suffering from shellshock, which in these days is better known as PTSD. I understand that he was buried alive for days, in a trench with shells exploding all around him.

Until the day he died he was affected by sudden loud noises, and in the event of a thunderstorm, he became extremely distressed. His wife Enid had to sit with him in a cupboard under the stairs, holding him whilst he shook uncontrollably until the storm was over.

Charles and Enid had a daughter called Jean. Jean married Ray and still lives in Darlington with her family. Ray sadly died some years ago.

As far as I know, Uncle Charlie never received any treatment for his condition, but when I read about some of the seemingly brutal treatments that were available, perhaps it was for the best.

My Uncle Robert was a wonderful man, known to me as Uncle Rob. Fortunately, for him, he was born with what they called 'flat feet'. This meant that he was rejected when he tried to join up to fight in the war. Evidently his condition meant that he wasn't suitable for marching in boots.

He was a great family man. Each Sunday he would ride on his bicycle to visit my Uncle Charlie and his family, and from there he would come to visit us. He was always happy and laughing, a real practical joker.

He and his wife Mary had four children; Gladys, Alice, Robert (Bobby) and Nancy. As cousins Bob (Bobby as I called him when I was a child) and I were very good friends throughout our lives.

Bob married Sheila and they had three children, Jeanette, Judith and Wendy. Sadly, Bob's marriage ended in divorce, but he did a magnificent job in raising all three daughters. All daughters married and Jeanette and Judith have their own families.

Gladys and Alice both married and raised families, sadly, both of them developed breast cancer and died when they were quite young. I remember when I was still a child listening to my Uncle Rob, talking to my mother about my cousin Gladys.

Gladys was serving in the navy in World War Two. She met and fell in love with a naval officer Jack who was due to be posted. They wanted to be married and she wanted her father's permission. Evidently my Uncle Rob was summoned to the office of Darlington waterworks for an important phone call. He had less than five minutes to make a decision as to whether to give his permission. The longest, and the shortest, five minutes of his life. He gave his permission, and fortunately, never lived to regret it. Jack was an absolute treasure.

Nancy, the youngest, married Arthur and they too had children. Sadly, Arthur died in 2004.

George was the youngest boy (too young to fight in the war). I understand he used to tease my mother mercilessly. My mother once relayed to me one of his most cruel tricks. As they lived on a farm, there were plenty of chickens wandering around the farmyard. One of them was particularly loved by my mother and evidently became quite a pet. One day when they were all sitting round the table and enjoying a roast chicken dinner, my Uncle George told my mother that they were eating her pet chicken. I'm sure that she eventually forgave him as they were always the best of friends when I knew them. George married Ruth, a bossy domineering woman, and they had one son called Brian. Brian was a good friend to me. I remember when I was very young and living in Richmond with my grandparents, on the occasions when he was on leave, he would visit me in his uniform and take me out for the day.

After I was married, we lost touch for quite a while. Years later, we were back in touch again. By this time, he was married to Freda and lived in Leeds. Sadly Freda died and a few years ago I lost touch with Brian once more. After a couple of years unsuccessfully trying to trace him, I can only conclude that he too must have died.

My mother was, on many occasions, kept home to work instead of going to school. Despite this, she did well in all subjects. She even learned basic French, including how to count, from her friendship with the daughter of a neighbour who attended a private school.

At one point, my grandfather's sister and family wanted to take my mother to Australia with them when she and her husband and sons went to live there. I understand my grandmother refused to let her go. The surname of the family was Lee. I can't remember the name of her husband, but the boys' names were Harold, Edgar, Vernon and Rupert. I understand that the family were quite successful in Australia, and Mr Lee ended up as the editor of a newspaper. That could be true, or it could be rumour, I have no way of knowing, though I have tried unsuccessfully many times to discover what happened to them. I believe that the city they settled in was Melbourne.

In later years things my mother told me built a picture of her childhood. When she was young they lived in a village near Darlington called Gainford. My grandfather worked as a farm labourer for the owners of Gainford Hall. He was a hard worker, much respected and appreciated by his employers.

I actually have a picture of him standing by some haystacks near Gainford Hall. He had just won 'Best Thatcher' for the stacks. I believe he also won competitions for ploughing the straightest furrow behind a horse and plough. He was a wonderful man – strict but fair. I am sure that my grandmother had also worked hard, but by the time my mother was born she had taken to drinking heavily.

As the youngest by many years, my mother took the brunt of my grandmother's drunken outbursts, sometimes necessitating her hiding in a small doll's rocking cradle, often for the entire night until the rages subsided.

With such memories of her own childhood it must have been very difficult for my mother to leave me to live with my grandparents, but I know she had no choice.

At that time my grandparents lived in a flat in Richmond, North Yorkshire. My grandfather had retired from farming, but had gone back to work helping to build a new parade ground at Catterick Camp. He felt that he was doing his bit to help the war effort.

The flat was at the bottom of a hill facing the main Market Square. The approach was via a very large bright blue door with a huge brass doorknob. To the right of the door was a butchers shop and to the left a greengrocers, both owned by a family, who I think also owned and rented out the flats above the shops. I think the name was Cherry, but after all this time

I could be mistaken. My mother became very friendly with the daughter of the family, a girl called Kathy. I remember she was always very kind to me.

The blue door, which was very heavy to open, led into a long, wide passageway. Straight ahead at the end of the passage another door opened outwards onto a flight of steps leading to the gardens.

The gardens were something special. They consisted of a series of walled gardens set in terraces, each one lower than the one before. Each terrace was surrounded by a high stone wall and each one had a door which opened into the one below. I think there were four terraces in total and the last opened directly onto Castle Walk. A magical place to play for a small girl, especially one with imagination.

On leaving the building, halfway down the first set of steps, on the right-hand side, was a door leading to a cellar. This was no ordinary cellar. The Cherry family had created a very comfortable air-raid shelter in case of attack from the air – this was most unlikely in Richmond.

In the cellar were beds and chairs – even blankets and pillows. It was to become my sanctuary – my own very secret place – but that was later.

At the end of the passage, to the right of the door leading to the garden, another door opened to reveal a staircase rising to the first floor, and thence to the second floor. My grandparents occupied the accommodation on the first floor.

At the front of the building were two bedrooms with windows looking up the cobbled square. I remember one could only access the second bedroom, which is where I slept, by going through the first. Across the landing to the rear of the building two steps led down to the kitchen, in the corner of which was the toilet. Beyond the kitchen was the living room, a lovely room with a welcoming fire and a huge bay window with far-reaching views across the river.

I slept in the second bedroom with familiar toys and things around me. I remember sometimes when crossing the landing to bed, I would meet people from the flat above coming up or going down the stairs.

Life was now very different. My grandmother was never the kind of person to give hugs and kisses. In fact I doubt very much that she ever really wanted me there.

My grandfather caught the bus to work each day. He returned each evening at the same time and got off the bus at the bus stop at the bottom of the hill.

One evening early in my stay, I was sent to meet him from the bus. I think my grandmother wanted to make sure that he came straight home! I remember this big, strong man, who looked so sad, getting off the bus. He looked down at me and said, "I see you've been sent to round me up!" Then he turned and started walking up the hill. After a few steps he stopped, turned, smiled and held out his hand saying, "I suppose we should look after one another." I still remember slipping my hand into his huge hand and feeling safe.

After that I met him every night from the bus and we walked hand in hand up the hill. I didn't go home from school. I waited for my grandfather. It was the only thing I looked forward to all day. I don't think my grandmother minded. The longer I played out the better she liked it. My grandfather however was my best friend and protector.

After tea every evening he would sit in a chair in front of the fire, and fill his pipe. I would often snuggle up, either on his knee or at his feet and just gaze at the fire, making pictures from the flames. My mother visited as often as she could. How l looked forward to her visit, and how sad I felt when she had to go.

I spent the days at school. I remember the classroom. We sat on benches, at long desks arranged in tiers. We wrote using chalk on slates, and at first things were good at school – my marks were good and I was even made chalk monitor!

Then one terrible day I went as usual to the bus stop and waited for the bus. The bus came but for the first time my grandfather was not on the bus. I went home. Kathy Cherry was waiting for me by the door. She had been crying. She told me that my grandad was poorly and home in bed.

My mother and uncles all arrived that night. Everyone was sad, most were in tears. I remember being allowed to see my grandad. He looked as though he was asleep. My granny was holding his hand and crying loudly. I was too young to realise that that was the last time I would see him.

Grandad passed away that night. I was told later that he had suffered a heart attack while trying to show young men how to wield a pick axe. I can vividly recall the sound of my grandmother crying and talking to him loudly during the night that he was laid out. I was in the next room. For all her faults in later years, I'm sure that my grandmother really loved him.

I also remember his funeral. He was buried in the cemetery in Reeth just outside Richmond.

After the funeral everyone went home and I was left to live alone with my grandmother.

3

My grandmother found it difficult to cope with the death of my grandfather. She began to spend a lot of time in The Castle, a pub halfway up the cobbled square. It became more and more obvious that I was an unwanted responsibility. I have no recollection of her ever slapping me or hitting me in any way, I'm sure she never did, but neither do I remember ever being able to talk to her. She obviously fed me but I have no memories of ever spending any quality time with her.

One of the first things I remember was that my grandmother removed all my toys, saying that I couldn't keep them tidy so I didn't deserve them. I was too afraid of the consequences to tell my mother.

We had to give up the bedrooms at the front of the building and live only in the big room at the back. I shared a bed with my grandmother in the corner of the room. I remember at the end of the bed, separating it from the rest of the room, stood a folding screen covered with Victorian scraps. I thought it was very beautiful and spent a lot of time looking at it, often spotting something I hadn't seen before, before I went to sleep.

My mother still visited as often as she could and somehow my grandmother managed to hide the extent of her drinking and present a caring front.

My mother would bring me new jumpers from time to time as well as shoes, skirts, etc. Each time, as soon as she had gone, they were taken from me and locked in a cupboard. "I'm not here to do your washing," Gran would say.

During the winter she made me wear the same two jumpers, alternating the one on top, week after week. They were never washed and I still remember the humiliation I felt on being told by a teacher that I needed to have my clothes washed.

This message was echoed by the other children in the class. Nobody wanted to sit next to me, and I used to long for school to end each day when I would be free. There was never any point in going home. Most times nobody would be there, and if they were, they had possibly had a drink, and would be easily annoyed. Fortunately Richmond is a lovely place surrounded by beautiful countryside.

I became very solitary and spent many hours each day exploring riverbanks, woodland paths, parks, streets and pathways, even the castle. The keeper at the castle came to recognise me and used to wave me through the gate without a ticket, when no one was looking.

After a while I knew every nook and cranny in the castle, every path through the woods, every bend in the river, all about Easby Abbey, every street and pathway in the town and when I was alone and exploring I think I was happy, especially during the long summer holidays.

There was of course always my secret place, the cellar. A place to escape to, when it was cold or raining, or when my grandmother was in a particularly bad mood. I still remember the fantasies I dreamt up in that place.

I must have lived in Richmond for about two years. I remember I had just moved to the junior school which was down a steep hill near to the station. I came home one day to find my mother and her friend Charles Harrison waiting for me. My mother had met Charles at work and he had visited on previous occasions. He was kind and I liked him. He also had the same name as my grandfather. I think Kathy Cherry had written to my mother expressing concern about my welfare. My bags were already packed, including all my confiscated toys and all the unworn clothes that she had brought me.

My grandmother was crying, trying to hug me, and saying she would miss me. I was overjoyed to be going home with my mother, but I remember feeling sorry for my grandmother. I was still only seven years old.

Leaving Richmond for a new life was a happy time, but despite everything I have happy memories of the time spent there.

I remember coming home with huge bunches of bluebells and cowslips, which in those days grew in profusion in woods and meadows. I remember watching rabbits and squirrels at play – they came so close I could almost touch them. I remember lying on a big flat stone by the river with my hand in the water tickling fish. I remember catching tadpoles in a jar, though I was made to take them back to the pond. I remember climbing to the top of tall trees. I remember climbing to the top of the castle tower from where I could see for miles.

I think those early years probably made me realise that whatever happened I could survive and look after myself.

My mother then had the task of finding a new home for us. She took me to live for a while with her brother, my uncle. Robert, Rob for short, his wife Mary, and their four children Gladys, Alice, Bobby and Nancy lived in a house which belonged to Darlington waterworks. The house was in the grounds of the waterworks with at least two reservoirs in the grounds. I shared a room with my cousins and went to the village school at High Coniscliffe.

It was a happy home. My Uncle Rob was one of the kindest men I have ever known with a great sense of fun. My Auntie Mary was a lovely person who was also a wonderful cook. Her cakes were second to none! My cousins were good to me, especially Bobby, and I repaid his kindness by always blaming him if anything went wrong! To this day we're good friends and he never bore a grudge. Those were good days. The only thing I recall I didn't like was the milk at school. For some reason the teacher used to warm the bottles on top of the stove. The smell was horrible, and whenever I hear certain hymns that we sang at school, I can still smell it!

I was warned many times of the dangers of the reservoirs, but having been so used to exploring on my own, I took little notice and ended up falling in. Luckily somebody saw me and pulled me out. I remember being severely reprimanded by the whole family. I had never seen my uncle so angry.

4

Because of the war most of the men were away fighting, thus leaving important and necessary jobs vacant. All over the country women were filling these vacancies. My mother filled one such vacancy. She left her job at the canteen and became a crane driver in North Road shops, building steam engines for the railway. The tracks for the crane ran along the roof of the factory. The job of the crane driver was to lift the very heavy pieces of the engine into position. My mother really enjoyed this job. The very last piece of an engine was the chimney, and when the time came for the chimney to be fitted, everyone stopped work to watch and cheer.

Obviously she now earned more money and was able to consider buying a property for us to live in. Few people had the courage to take out a mortgage in those days, especially single parents. Women in my mother's position as a divorcee were not looked upon kindly. However, she was determined to provide a home for us and therefore we moved into a small terraced house, namely number 70 Reid Street.

This was to be our home for many years to come.

Number 70 Reid Street was a typical two-up-two-down terraced house. There were two rooms downstairs, one at the front and one at the back divided by a staircase leading up to two bedrooms, one front and one back. The front door was straight off the street and entered into a small porch which in turn led to the front room with its bay window and fireplace. Above the fireplace were two wall lights supplied by gas. The back room had a door leading to the backyard and a cupboard which went under the stairs. A gas cooker stood at one end of the room, whilst at the other end was a deep square sink with a cold water tap. Next to the sink across the corner was a large concrete slab. In the centre of the slab a circular metal lid lifted to reveal a deep metal bowl. Beneath this was a small grate where a fire could be lit to heat water in the bowl above. In the backyard, next to the back door, a large tin bath hung on the wall. Across the yard was the toilet and next to that was the coal house. A gate in the wall led to the back alley, used by bin men to empty bins and coal men to deliver coal.

My mum slept in the front room and I had the back room. I remember being so excited to have my own room again.

Across the road at the front was a school – Reid Street School. The entrance was exactly opposite our front door so there was no danger of me getting lost this time!

My mother worked long hours, 7am to 7pm and sometimes nightshifts which were 7pm to 7am. I became a latchkey child. There were many others in those days. I wore the house key on a string round my neck.

Life was hard for my mum. Each morning she prepared my breakfast and left it on the table for me. An alarm woke me in time for me to eat my breakfast, clean my teeth and dress, before crossing the road to school. I also had food prepared and left for me for when I came in from school. When my mother came home from work after a twelve-hour shift, she cooked supper and tucked me up in bed.

Bath time in those days was probably only once a week as it entailed carrying the heavy tin bath into the house, heating water in the bowl in the kitchen and carrying it to fill the bath. It took a long time to heat the water and carry it a jug at a time to fill the tin bath.

My mother used to place the bath in front of a roaring fire in the front room. Around it she stood two tall clothes horses on which she hung blankets. This provided a very cosy place to have a bath. When I had finished she would have a bath herself, but then had the task of emptying the bath and carrying it back to the yard.

I still remember those baths. When all was finished I would sit on my mother's knee with a hot drink before being tucked up in bed. For the rest of the week, a daily strip wash had to suffice.

At some point while we lived in this house my mother earned enough money to have electricity installed, so we now had electric lights. She also had a small extension built at the back of the kitchen. This meant that the tin bath could now be housed inside, and things like bicycles stored more easily. We still had to cross the yard to use the toilet even in thick snow. Behind the toilet door hung my sledge, much used in the winter months!

I always had nice clean clothes and I ate lunch at school. School began at 9am and finished at 4:30pm. I made friends at school and also had friends in the same street. Next door lived Brenda and Jimmy. Next door to the other side lived Leslie and four doors up lived David. Leslie also only had his mum. I think his father died fighting in the war. I have many memories of the years we lived in that house, though I can't guarantee to relate them in the right order.

I restarted Reid Street School, this time in the juniors. I remember doing well at school and usually achieved top marks in most subjects. There was a boy called Gerald who came top in most things, especially arithmetic. I was usually second! I never managed to beat him in arithmetic! My favourite teacher was Miss James. She was my teacher for the last two years at junior school. Miss James was engaged to a man who was away fighting in the war. She often held us spellbound as she relayed stories about his exploits. I never knew what happened to him. I really hope he came back from the war. She was a lovely lady, really kind to me. She always tried to convince me that I could do really well as long as I believed in myself.

Lunch was eaten in the school hall at long tables and I seem to remember it was reasonably okay.

That is all except some 'orange jam', which I thought tasted vile. I remember one occasion when I was given a large helping of this jam even though I had asked not to have it. Policy was that everything on our plates should be eaten! I refused to eat this jam! I was told that I would stay there until I did eat it. I still remember sitting all alone in the hail, the plate with the jam in front of me. I stubbornly refused to eat it. I sat there late into the afternoon, it must have been wintertime as I remember it began to get dark. I cannot for the life of me remember the outcome but obviously I was allowed to leave the table and go home eventually. One thing I do know is that I did not eat the jam. The experience must have had quite an effect on me as I remember in later years when reading *Jane Eyre*, one particular chapter made me think of the time I sat alone in the school hall for a whole afternoon.

In the fourth year juniors we all sat a test (later known as the eleven-plus) to determine which school we would move onto. Because of high numbers in Reid Street School some of us had to move to the girls' secondary school, a building next door to ours, for the latter part of the summer term. I hated the time spent at that school and I remember praying every night that I would pass my scholarship and therefore go to the girls' grammar school. Luckily I did, as did my best friend Ann Hislop. I still remember how happy Ann and I felt as we broke up for the summer holidays and left that school for good. It wasn't the teachers we hated, but we had nothing at all in common with the girls who went to that school.

Friends at this time were, in the main, neighbours, for example Brenda and Jimmy. Brenda was a year younger than me, and Jimmy a couple of years older. Brenda's mum and Brenda used to sleep with me in my house on the occasions when my mum had to work nightshifts.

Jimmy could be a bit of a bully and at times I was the target of his bullying. My mother told me that I was the only one who could teach him not to bully me. In other words I should stand up to him. I don't think she actually advocated violence but one day I went out to play and he was sitting on the school wall opposite. I should explain that the school wall itself was quite low. Before the war, tall iron railings were set into the wall, but these had all been removed because of the war effort. He started to taunt me about something and I hit him – so hard it knocked him off the wall. Strange to say he never bothered me again.

Ann was my friend at school, but she lived a considerable way from school, so at that time we didn't really get together after school. I sometimes went to play with a girl called Stella who lived in a big house not too far away. I occasionally spent time with twins who lived in the next street. I remember their mother wore lots of make-up and very low tops. I don't think many people approved.

But on the whole in those early years most of my time was spent with Brenda, Jimmy, David and Leslie. We spent hours playing in the local park, the street, the school playground or even indoors.

One year I had a Monopoly game for Christmas (I still have it). I remember we played every day for weeks and weeks and I was the envy of my friends. How times have changed… a Monopoly game would probably be a stocking filler these days! Yet to me, back then, it was a wonderful gift, and I still treasure it.

Later when I went to the grammar school I made new friends Sheila, Elizabeth, Marjorie and many others.

5

If the weather was fine we were always outdoors. The favourite place was the Dene. This was parkland formed by a stream flowing through the centre with banks, sometimes steep, rising on either side. There was a series of these small parks which were crossed at intervals by roads. Some were cultivated with flowers and shrubs, one included a tennis court, but the one closest to us had swings, slides, roundabouts, seesaws and a climbing frame.

I was very much a tomboy. If there was a tree to be climbed I would climb it, and if there was a stream to fall in, I would fall into it. Occasions when my limbs were not adorned with sticking plasters or bandages were few and far between.

We played games in the street and in the school yard opposite after school, which included hide-and-seek and tag. We also played skipping games. This involved a long rope being turned by a person at each end whilst one, two or more skipped in the centre, usually to a rhyme.

Most of the rhymes have long since disappeared from my memory, apart from one, and I can only remember the first two lines of that. It went something like, '*See them in their Russian boots, Russian boots. With their garters hanging loose, hanging loose'.* I'm sure there were other rhymes about Germans and Hitler as well.

Other games included singing games, for example, 'The Farmer's in His Den'. Many hours could be spent playing games with a ball up against a wall, often to well-known rhymes or set patterns.

I remember having a small ball with four dice-shaped blocks. I would spend hours trying to complete set routines, picking up, putting down and moving the blocks while bouncing and catching a ball. This game was called checks.

One of our favourite games was called 'Johnny Shine a Light'. This involved using a torch. Looking back I'm sure that we would have been in trouble if the air-raid warden had ever found us playing. Blackout rules came into force at dusk! Fortunately I don't think Darlington was anywhere near the top of Hitler's hit list.

We used to play in the school yard and the surrounding area. But we could only play after it got dark. We all had a torch. All but one of us had to hide. One person started as the searcher. As you were caught you joined in as a searcher. The winner was the last one to be caught. Searchers were allowed to ask somebody by name to 'shine a light'. A torch was flashed once, very briefly. The person who shone the light could then quickly run to hide somewhere else. The game quickly became chaotic, but great fun.

However, it almost ended in disaster for me one night! There were just two of us left to catch. I was running across the playground, looking behind me trying to evade capture. In the middle of the playground were some metal climbing frames. Evidently I hit one with a bang and dropped like a stone. The first thing I remember was opening my eyes to see four very frightened faces looking down at me: Brenda, Jimmy, David and Leslie. I think they all thought I was dead!

The seasons often dictated which games were played and when. Winter was often severe in the north-east and every year we had snow, sometimes very deep.

In those days people would always clear the pathway outside their homes and the snow would be piled up in the gutter. The roads were never cleared. I suppose they didn't need to be as there were so few cars around.

I think I said earlier that we all had a sledge. Mine was hanging behind the toilet door across the backyard. We had such fun pulling one another up and down the street until the snow was so packed that it was dangerous to walk on. We also went to the Dene, where, because of the sloping banks, we had great fun sledging downhill.

I remember we stayed out in the snow until our hands and feet became numb with cold. We would then go indoors to warm up. The pain we felt as our hands and feet thawed out was agonising, but once we had warmed up with dry socks and dry gloves, we went out again to repeat the process over and over until it was time for bed.

Bonfire night was unknown to us in those days because of the war. There was a blackout in force after dark and no lights of any kind were allowed to be shown. Hence the banning of bonfires and fireworks. However, 'Mischief night', which I now presume to be Halloween, was popular.

The street where we lived was built as a terrace of flat-fronted houses with two doors side by side. A favourite trick was to tie the two handles of the doors together. Then someone would knock on both doors and we would all hide across the road behind the school wall to watch as both occupants tried to open their doors.

Another favourite, which I think Leslie initiated, involved a reel of black cotton, a drawing pin and a button. The button was attached to the cotton about six inches away from a drawing pin which was also tied to the cotton. The drawing pin was then pushed into the window frame while the reel of cotton was unwound across the road. Then, with everyone safely concealed behind the wall, the button would be tapped on the glass.

6

As my mother worked long hours including Saturdays, it was necessary for me to help by doing the weekly shop. At the top of the street around the corner were two or three small local shops. A bread shop, a small grocers and a newsagents. These were used when small items, for example a loaf of bread or a bottle of milk, were needed. A weekly shop however necessitated a trip into Darlington town centre.

There, in the street called Priestgate, was the Co-op. On the left-hand side of the street was the grocers, and on the right the butchers.

Once a week I walked into town carrying a purse holding money, and a list. I called first at the butchers where I purchased a fillet of lamb, this being the top half of the leg. I then crossed the road to the grocers where I handed them my list. My list included the basics: tea, sugar, butter and eggs etc. I remember watching them cut the butter from a large slab. It was then patted into shape using two wooden implements, and the process ended by pressing a pattern on top of the block of butter before it was neatly wrapped in greaseproof paper. Other items were weighed and placed in paper bags. At that time most foods were rationed so the amounts I could buy depended on how many coupons we had.

All the goods I bought were packed into my baskets and then I paid for them. This was the most exciting part for me. My money was placed into a small container which was then attached to wires which ran from the counter up to an office high above the shop. The shop assistant then pulled a lever which sent the money shooting up to the office along the wires. There were three or four sets of wires and I remember watching to see when a hand would reach up to take my container and then send my change back down to me. Back then we had a number with the Co-op, called a dividend number, which collected small amounts of money each time you shopped. I think our number was 34289, but I could be wrong as it is a long time ago.

On some occasions, I was lucky enough to see some of the delivery wagons entering or leaving the Co-op premises. These were pulled by the most magnificent shire horses. I loved to watch these huge gentle giants as they performed their daily tasks.

My friend Ann used to help to groom these magnificent creatures (possibly they were stabled near to the police horses). I can still recall her distress when they were retired, and the job they had performed so successfully over the years was taken over by vans. Suddenly, it seemed almost overnight, horses disappeared from our roads, but I remember with great fondness, horses pulling wagons to deliver our milk and our coal. I even remember milk being delivered in huge urns, in a trap pulled by a pony. The milk was then ladled into our own jugs. I think that was when we were living in Parkside. I also recall the days when children would be sent out with a shovel to scoop up horse manure for the garden.

But back to my shopping. Carrying my shopping, I then walked up to High Row where I caught a trolleybus to take me back home. Trolleybuses were a single decker with a door in the centre of the bus, powered by electricity fed through a long pole which was connected to wires high above the street. The trolleybus took me closer to home but there was still quite a walk to get to my house.

From time to time, usually on a Sunday, we went back to Richmond to see my grandmother and check to see if she was okay. We used to do her shopping and any other jobs she needed doing.

I can't remember exactly when, but I think I was probably about nine years old when I started travelling to Richmond alone each Saturday to do her shopping. I shopped in a shop called Liptons halfway up the Market Square. I remember feeling sorry for her and I worried about her being on her own.

7

As I stated previously my mother worked long hours, often twelve hours a day, six days a week. There were few perks to her job, but one was the availability of privilege tickets on the railway, including two free passes per year for my mother and for me.

Privilege tickets meant a reduction in the price of a rail ticket, but the free passes meant that we could go anywhere in the country for free. Each year my mum took advantage of these passes and took us on holiday twice a year. Each year we had a week in Brighton and a few days in Edinburgh.

In Brighton we stayed in a B&B just off the seafront. Each morning before breakfast I would go down to the sea, picking my way painfully across the pebble beach for a quick dip in the water before going back for breakfast. The first night of the holiday was always spent visiting various theatres in order to book a show for the coming week. In those days many London shows visited Brighton.

During the day we visited neighbouring towns, spent time on the two piers where I loved driving the racing cars, and enjoyed walking on the South Downs.

One year, whilst we were there, we were exploring the Lanes, a well-known and popular area full of interesting little shops. We discovered a bric-a-brac shop and in the window was a weather house.

It was beautifully detailed, and I remember thinking it was one of the most beautiful things I had ever seen. It was designed in the form of a Swiss chalet. The upstairs windows had shutters and balconies and inside the windows hung gingham curtains. Window boxes were filled with beautiful artificial flowers and bougainvillea climbed the walls from pots on the ground.

There were two doors at the front. When it was sunny, a girl, dressed in Swiss national costume, came out of the door on the left, and when it was raining, a boy, dressed in Swiss national costume came out of the door on the right, and when it was neither one thing nor the other, both hovered in their doorways. I fell in love with it and I wanted to buy it.

We approached the door of the shop, though I think we knew that it would be far too expensive for us to afford. The shop was closed, I remember being really disappointed, so it was decided that we would return the following day.

Each day we found time to retrace our steps to the same shop, and each day we found it closed. The day before we were due to leave, we went again to the shop, and this time to my utter joy, it was open.

We really need not have worried as to whether we could afford the weather house because we were told it was not for sale. Display only. Perhaps that was the best outcome because I'm sure we couldn't have afforded it anyway.

I do know that my mother bought me a small weather house from a different shop. I actually still have it.

Before the theatre in the evenings we went for a meal to a local restaurant a few streets away from the B&B. Although there was quite an extensive menu I remember that I usually chose the same thing. Sausage, egg, chips and tomato. It was the first time I had ever had tomatoes cut across and grilled in that way, and I loved them. The sausages I remember were delicious. Sometimes Mr Harrison came with us and I still remember the wonderful times we had.

Our visits to Edinburgh were also exciting. Once more we slept in a B&B. We visited Edinburgh Castle, Holyrood House, Portobello on the coast where I rode on roundabouts and enjoyed all the fun of the fair. We walked along Princes Street and climbed to the top of Arthur's Seat.

On one occasion we took Brenda with us. Brenda's mother often took me to the seaside at Redcar during the school holidays whilst my mother was at work, so this was my mother's way of repaying her.

I remember the trips to Redcar quite clearly. We went on a bus from Darlington. The bus had to pass through Middlesbrough, a town which I remember was grey, dismal and grimy. The days at the seaside were fun, though I remember one occasion when I was wearing a knitted swimsuit. This was fine whilst I was digging in the sand, but not so fine when I went into the sea and it got wet and stretched!

When my mother had days off we often went for walks and picnics. One day each year we took baskets, boarded a bus and went to a special woodland where we collected blackberries. The jam and pies that resulted from such visits were mouth-watering and I can still taste them. Sadly one year we visited the same woodland, and had actually left the bus, before we realised that all the trees had been cut down so there were no blackberries to pick!

From time to time we enjoyed day trips to places like Whitby and Scarborough, and on one occasion I remember we even ventured as far as Bridlington.

8

During my time at Reid Street, Miss Lillian Thompson visited our house. Before she was married my mother had been in service to Mrs Thompson. Her daughter was Lillian Thompson. Lillian became very fond of my mother and wrote to her several times each year. Each Christmas she enclosed a gift of £10.

The occasion on which she visited Reid Street was to bring me a gift.

The gift was the most beautiful black Scottish terrier. She had a wonderful pedigree, and we called her Bunty. She was a lovely dog, even though she ate all my coloured pencils and chewed many other items whilst she was a young puppy. We bought her a red tartan collar which looked very smart against her shiny black coat.

One day my mother had just bathed her and she looked gorgeous. I was allowed to take her for a walk with strict instructions as to where to go.

The night before this, a German plane had flown very low down the main road in town, strafing the police station with its guns as it went. This was something that all my friends wanted to see. They persuaded me to go with them and I went, totally ignoring all my instructions.

On the way to the police station we had to pass through North Lodge Park where I let Bunty off the lead. As we reached the gate at the other end of the park everybody got very excited. Across the road, which was a main road, the police station came into view and the bullet holes were very apparent. We all rushed across the road to get a closer look. What followed remains with me to this day.

I had forgotten all about my dog who had run after me, and the double-decker bus which was passing at the time was unable to stop. It still seems like a bad dream, turning round, seeing somebody carrying my dog to the side of the road and a policeman standing there. He was very kind – he gave me her tartan collar which I carried, crying and totally inconsolable, all the way home. My mother knew something dreadful had happened as soon as I walked through the door. To this day I feel so guilty.

I learnt the hard way of the awful consequences disobedience can have. I think I cried for days, partly from grief and partly from guilt.

The following year my Uncle George visited.

He was a farmer at the time, though he later turned his hand to landscape gardening. He had with him a beautiful collie dog, a Border collie who, he told us, was to be destroyed because the farmer who owned her didn't want to keep her.

Obviously we fell in love with her and kept her. Shortly afterwards we realised why he didn't want to keep her, though we couldn't comprehend his decision!

We arrived home one day to find Floss, which was her name, had given birth to six pups. They were beautiful dogs and eventually we found good homes for them all.

Floss was a wonderful dog. In the early years when I was very young she was closer to my mother, but as I grew into my teens she became my constant companion. I even had a cardboard box fitted to the rear of my bicycle. If I was going out somewhere I just asked her if she wanted to come, and she immediately leapt into the box and sat there as good as gold until I reached my destination and was told to get down. She was the most obedient dog and never needed to be kept on the lead apart from if she saw anybody with a ladder, there was no holding her back.

On more than one occasion we had to rescue our window cleaner. He was up the ladder and Floss had climbed the bottom two rungs and was barking and growling furiously. We can only assume that somebody who used a ladder had at one time treated her badly, possibly kicked her. Fortunately we did not encounter too many people with ladders when we were out walking, or especially when she was riding pillion on the back of my bicycle.

I can still remember the day I had my first bicycle. I think it was probably bought to celebrate the fact that I had passed my eleven-plus and was going to Darlington High School for Girls. It was bought for me by Charles Harrison, my mother's friend. I don't think my mother would have been able to afford to buy it for me. I was unaware of what was about to happen, when one day we walked into town and visited a cycle shop on Northgate. I will never forget the excitement I felt as I left the shop, the proud owner of a beautiful, shiny, brand-new, Royal Enfield cycle. (It was my pride and joy and remained so until the summer of 1953 when Derek accompanied me to a shop to trade it in for a racing bike.)

I can't remember learning to ride a bicycle, or even owning bicycles that I must have ridden previously. But I will never forget riding home on that new bike. I was allowed to go ahead whilst Charles and my mother walked home. I must have appeared a real show-off as I showed off my bike to everybody I came into contact with, especially to Brenda, Jimmy, David and Leslie.

9

One day, I can't remember exactly when, though I know it was before I became the proud owner of my new bicycle, and whilst I was still attending primary school, a rather large piece of furniture was delivered to our little house. It was a beautiful upright piano. It took pride of place in the front room, near the window, angled across the corner. Soon after that, my mother arranged piano lessons for me.

The piano teacher was a dapper little man who worked in a solicitor's office during the day, and taught pupils how to play the piano on evenings and weekends. I think his name was Mr Thornton, but I could be confusing it with the street where he lived which was Thornton Street. Therefore I shall refer to him as Mr T. I think my mother met him when she had occasion to use the solicitors, probably when she was buying Reid Street.

I used to visit his house, once a week at about seven o'clock, for one hour's tuition. He lived in a street of terraced houses, probably just under half a mile away from where I lived.

Walking there in the summer was no problem. However, in the winter time it was dark and because of the war there were no street lights. Sometimes the moon made up for the lack of street lights, but on the night when clouds covered the moon, it was very dark.

I used to run, like the wind, keeping to the centre of the road away from houses, gardens, alleyways, in fact, anywhere where I thought someone might jump out and grab me. Fortunately, there were few cars back then, so there was little danger of being hit by one!

Learning to play the piano was a wonderful opportunity for me, one which years later, I regretted not taking full advantage of. Yes, I practised! I probably drove the neighbours mad, especially when I had to practise scales and chords.

Much later at the end of my first year at high school, I was ecstatic when I was allowed to play my first tune. I had music given to me by Mr T, and also a little book containing all the music from the film *Bambi* had appeared under the Christmas tree from Father Christmas. Easy to guess which was my favourite?

At the end of school term, those of us who were learning to play a musical instrument were expected to show off our talents by playing before the whole class. Mr T had picked out a delightful little tune which we practised for weeks leading up to the end-of-term performance. However, I thought I knew best and decided to play one of the tunes from my *Bambi* book!

I can still visualise the scene.

A beautiful grand piano took pride of place on a raised platform at the end of the school hall. When my turn came, I nervously seated myself on the piano stool and made a complete hash of it. I still remember how embarrassed I felt. I never did tell Mr T what I had done.

I suppose my heart was never really in it. I didn't realise then the advantages playing the piano would have afforded me in my career later on.

Also, I really wanted to dance. For a while I attended classes at a local dance school. However, most of my time at that school was spent sitting on a bench with another little girl, watching specially chosen girls practise in preparation for performances undertaken at various venues in the area. When my mother discovered this, she stopped sending me for lessons. After all, she was struggling to pay for them.

Looking back, I suspect that the other little girl was from the same sort of background as me. In other words, we didn't have a lot of money and nor did we fit in.

10

During the war we were all issued with a gas mask. I think we were supposed to carry them everywhere with us. Each mask came in a cardboard box with a long string attached so that we could hang it on our shoulders. Every now and again at school, we had to practise putting our masks on. We all hated it. The masks were horrible. They smelt strongly of rubber and once put on, they clamped themselves to your face like a limpet. The rectangular piece of Perspex, obviously there so that you could see where you were going, misted up almost immediately!

It was soon discovered that by blowing into your gas mask you could actually blow raspberries, a sound caused when air escaped between the rubber and the cheeks. Some of the boys realised that if you blew really hard you could make loud farting noises. The whole class would then dissolve into fits of giggles and a very flustered teacher would instruct us to remove the masks at once. As time went on, gas mask practice became less frequent.

Besides taking precautions against a possible gas attack, there was also the threat of bombs being dropped. All over the country people began building their own defences, mainly in the shape of bomb shelters in their back garden. Most of these were Anderson shelters. These consisted of sheets of corrugated iron, half buried in the ground and bent over at the top in a curve and bolted together.

The corrugated iron above the ground was then covered with soil, and the space between the lower sections was dug out to create a place to shelter during air raids. At the first sight of approaching enemy aircraft each town and city sounded a siren, or sirens, to warn of the danger. We occasionally stayed with Nell Stephenson at the beginning of the war and I vaguely remember being woken during the night, wrapped in a blanket and carried downstairs, outside, and into the Anderson shelter where we stayed until the next siren sounded the all-clear. Two very distinctive sounds I shall never forget. To this day, that warning sound of an air raid still brings back that feeling of uncertainty and unease.

However, another sound brought a feeling of hope. I remember vividly hearing the voice of Winston Churchill coming through a somewhat crackly wireless that we had back then. This was the voice of the man who was keeping us all safe. Well to me it was, and also to millions of others. His was the voice which brought comfort and hope to so many. His was the voice that made me feel safe.

At ten years old, I had no conception of politics, and I still remember the anger and confusion I felt as the whole country seemingly turned against him in July 1945, and voted him out.

Another sound which sticks in my memory from way back then is the song 'You Are My Sunshine'. Everybody seemed to be singing it.

Of course, another voice will always be remembered from those years, a voice which brought hope to all of us, not only those of us at home, listening on the radio, but also to all the young men and women fighting overseas for our freedom. Vera Lynn.

Her songs will last forever. As children, we enjoyed singing along, but we were far too young to appreciate the meaning of the words that were being sung. Words that have had such meaning on many more occasions since.

It was cold in the shelters, and because they were below ground they often filled up with rainwater. Fortunately Darlington was not targeted very often, and by the time we lived in Reid Street we sheltered in the cupboard under the stairs if and when there was an air raid.

Years later, when I met Derek, I learned of a very different kind of war people in cities endured. Manchester was one of the cities that took a dreadful battering night after night after night. At that time Derek lived in Stockport on the outskirts of Manchester. He remembers having to go into the Anderson shelter nearly every evening. He also remembers the vivid glow in the sky every night as fires raged out of control all over the city.

Derek's father, Alf, volunteered as an air-raid warden. Wardens used to patrol the area, to make sure no lights were showing and to help people who needed assistance, and many other necessary tasks. Derek often related an amusing tale about his dad. Evidently one evening as Alf was patrolling, everyone was safely in their Anderson shelters, when he heard the whistling sound of a bomb dropping close by. He dived headfirst into the nearest Anderson shelter hoping it would give him some sort of cover. Unfortunately for him it was full of water! Derek said it took his dad a long time to live that one down.

I should mention food rationing.

We all had coupons, each one allocated to a different type of food. Once we had used these coupons we were unable to obtain that particular item again until our next coupons became valid. We never went hungry though.

My Uncle Charlie turned the whole of his garden into a vegetable plot. He grew everything that was possible to grow. We never went short of green vegetables, especially cabbages. At that time Uncle Charlie lived with his wife Enid and their daughter Jean, who is quite a bit older than me, in a smart semi-detached property on Brinkburn Drive in Darlington. Every so often I would visit them, always taking a basket with me, and I would return, usually with a cabbage, but sometimes with a basket full of freshly picked garden peas still in their pods. I loved the peas and would often start eating them on the way home. I remember there was a knack to getting it just right. This meant putting pressure on the pod in exactly the right place. It would then snap open to reveal a row of juicy green peas. Delicious. However, one day I opened a peapod to reveal a row of exceptionally large juicy peas.

I was just about to pop them into my mouth when I noticed a hole in one of the peas. Emerging from this hole was a large green caterpillar. Needless to say I don't think I ever ate peas straight from the pod again without thorough investigation.

Uncle Charlie also built a large wooden frame in his garden upon which he grew sweet peas. They were beautiful and the perfume was exquisite. Auntie Enid often cut me a large bunch to take home with me and I still remember the perfume that filled our small house.

One thing that was never rationed during the war was bread. I seem to remember that bread was rationed after the war ended because of a shortage of wheat. I believe that meat was the last thing to come off ration, and that was in 1954, the year before I was married.

But back to bread.

I used to visit a shop on the corner of a nearby street to buy bread. Sometimes it was still warm, having just been delivered by a local baker. It was delicious, especially whilst it was still hot. On one occasion, which I remember vividly, I chewed off all four corners of the loaf before reaching home. My mother unwrapped the loaf and asked me why the corners looked as though they had been chewed. I said that they were like that when I bought it.

Looking back I think my mother was very clever. She didn't get angry, she just rewrapped the loaf and told me to put on my coat and take it back to the shop, and that I was to tell them we did not want a loaf with chewed corners. She then handed me the loaf, held open the front door for me to leave and then closed it behind me.

I don't know how long I stood outside our house, knowing that I could not go back to the shop, but not knowing how on earth I was going to get out of this one. Eventually I had to go back in, and I had to confess that I had chewed the corners of the loaf and that I had lied about it. I learnt two very important things that day, one was that all actions have consequences, and two that it is very wrong to lie.

Another day that I remember vividly was the day when I answered the door to a homeless man. He was tall, with long unkempt hair and a long shaggy grey beard. His clothes were ragged and unwashed. In those days all homeless people were referred to as tramps. I must have recoiled in shock on seeing him as he said he was sorry to have startled me and was my mother at home, and if she was did she have any food to spare. I think I said something like, "I'm sorry," and I closed the door quickly.

After he had gone I started to think how terrible it must be not to have a home and not to have any food. I remember going to the pantry which was under the stairs and all I could find was a packet of digestive biscuits and two tomatoes. I grabbed them and rushed out of the house. I looked up and down the street but I couldn't see him anywhere. I started to run down the street and remember feeling that it was vital that I found him because he had no food. I eventually saw him walking down an alleyway. I remember racing up to him and offering him the two tomatoes and the unopened packet of digestive biscuits. He looked at me and said, "Did your mother send me these? Does she know you have brought them to me?" Without hesitation I answered, "Yes she does!" I know it was a lie but I reckoned God would not mind under the circumstances. I then thrust them into his hands, turned and ran home as fast as I could. That night when she came home I told her what I had done.

During the war we had a local policeman who was responsible for most things in our area, such as keeping the peace, checking on blackouts etc. They were usually on foot but many had a bicycle as well. One day I was walking down the street, probably daydreaming as usual, and for some reason I was carrying a piece of paper. As I walked I was tearing this piece of paper into tiny pieces like confetti, and I clutched these tiny pieces tightly in my hand.

Again for some unknown reason as I approached a lamppost I grabbed it with one hand and I decided to swing around it, and as I swung I threw the confetti up over my head and each tiny piece floated slowly down to the road beneath.

Suddenly into my view as I was swinging round the lamppost came a bicycle wheel and at each side of this bicycle wheel were two black boots. I stopped swinging and my eyes slowly raised up from the ground and bit by bit in front of me grew the vision of a very tall, very stern-looking policeman. He was still sitting astride his very large bicycle, arms folded, with his feet firmly planted on the ground. I remember he didn't say a word. He simply shook his head, looked at me and then at all the pieces of paper on the floor, then back at me again, then once more to all the pieces of paper on the floor. I didn't say a word back. I just knew what I had to do. So I immediately got down on the floor and picked up every single piece of paper that I had dropped. When I had picked up the very last one I stuffed them all into my pocket. Then and only then did I make eye contact with the policeman. He nodded his head and said, "Don't ever do that again," and with that he slowly mounted his bicycle and rode off down the street. In those days most of us respected policemen and what they stood for.

I seem to remember the shop facing the top of our street was a newsagents. I can't remember at what age I became a regular reader of *Girls' Crystal*, a story paper for girls, but I remember each week waiting excitedly for the next edition. Most of the stories were in serial form and I just couldn't wait each week to find out what had happened.

All the good things seemed to happen at once when I was eleven years old. That was 1945 and what a year it was. My dream came true and I started to attend Darlington High School for Girls, and even better than that... the war came to an end!

All over the country people held street parties to celebrate. I vaguely remember attending a celebration which was held at the lower end of the street.

Reid Street was split into two. The bottom half of the street consisted of flat-fronted terraced houses on either side of the street. There was then a small gap where an alleyway branched off on either side. The top end of the street, which is where I lived, consisted of a row of terraced bay-windowed houses on one side of the road and the school on the other.

As children we didn't really understand what was going on, but I believe that initially the bottom end of the street did not want to include those of us who lived at the top end. I have no idea why. I know I attended but I can't really remember very much about it. All I do know is that everyone was happy!

Of course the end of the war heralded the return of the Saturday cinema. Every Saturday morning hordes of children from all over the town descended on the various cinemas in the town centre. I think it cost three pence to sit downstairs, but each Saturday I was given the princely sum of sixpence which enabled me to sit upstairs, often in the front row.

I know we watched a variety of films – a mixture of comedy, cartoons, and serialised films of heroes such as *Flash Gordon, Roy Rogers* and lots more.

Cowboys were very popular at that time and many of the films depicted scenes of cowboys being ambushed by hundreds of Apache and Sioux. Hence, after the film show, we left the cinema and most of the little boys took on the character of either a cowboy or an Apache.

11

A new school meant new friends and slowly but surely the times I spent with Brenda, Jimmy, David and Leslie became few and far between.

I was now able to cycle to see new friends after school. Together we cycled to nearby villages and parks, but mainly we visited a certain spot on the river where a bend created a small pebbly beach. The river at this point flowed quite slowly but it was shallow and therefore quite safe to paddle. On the opposite bank however, on the inside bend, erosion had created a deep pool. It was a wonderful place to swim and play. As time went on I became more adventurous on my bike – I had a bike rack fitted to the back, where my mother helped me to fix the cardboard box so that I could take our beautiful Border collie everywhere I went. She loved our visits to the river.

I was now attending a new school. No longer just across the road, but over a mile and a half away. I walked there and back every day, rain or shine… sadly we were not allowed to cycle to school.

I now had to wear a uniform. This consisted of a navy blue gymslip, over a long-sleeved, square-necked white shirt.

During the winter we wore a navy-blue gabardine raincoat and a navy-blue felt hat adorned with a ribbon made up of the school's colours. I remember wearing black shoes, which were polished so vigorously that you really could see your face in them. During the winter time I also wore long woollen stockings. I remember they used to itch!

In the summertime we wore gingham dresses. The colour depended on the house you had been allocated when you started the school. My house was Caedman and our colour was lilac. We also wore white socks and brown buckled sandals. If we so wished we could wear a straw boater or Panama instead of the felt hat in the summer. I think in the early years of starting school most opted to discard the felt hat in favour of the boater in the summer months. However, it only took one heavy rain storm to turn a once smart boater into a soggy straw mess. Hence by the time I reached the upper fourth, there were very few to be seen in my year. For the girls who came from my kind of background, it was impossible to afford to replace them every time they got wet.

The first weeks, or even months, of attending this new school meant 'running the gauntlet' to and from school each day. We had to learn to ignore the jibes and comments shouted at us as we walked to school. Nothing really bad, but 'high school snob' or 'why are you wearing a silly hat?' were the type of comments. I didn't care. I was going to the school I wanted to go to.

I soon settled in at school and became accustomed to a new way of teaching. Each day started with registration in our form room with our form teacher who was responsible for our pastoral care. After that we followed our timetable and moved from classroom to laboratory and from art room to gymnasium depending on whatever subject we were studying. Most subjects were new to the majority of us. French and chemistry to name but two. I was particularly happy because now I could spend the majority of my time with my friend Ann.

We ate lunch at school, and one day after lunch, before we started the afternoon session, Ann and I explored the school grounds. We discovered a set of rabbit hutches, four in total. They were built in tiers, two above two, standing on legs which raised them up off the ground. We both had a love of small animals and immediately made enquiries as to whether we could keep rabbits.

We were delighted when we were given permission to keep rabbits and it wasn't long before I was the proud owner of a beautifully marked black and white Dutch rabbit named Floppy. Ann chose a female, also a black and white Dutch rabbit, but I can't for the life of me remember what she called it.

This all happened in the summertime and as winter approached we worried we would have to possibly keep our rabbits at home. However, luck was on our side.

In another part of the grounds was a small garden shed with a window to one side, fully waterproof and windproof, standing empty and unused. After pleading our case we were allowed to move our rabbits into the shed. Of course this meant we could get even more animals, which we did. If my memory serves me right, Ann ended up with two rabbits and a guinea pig and l ended up with two rabbits and two mice.

The hut was kept locked when we were not there. There were at least three keys: Ann had one, I had one, and one was kept in the office. One morning we arrived early as usual to check that everything was okay and to top up water. We were horrified at what we found. Someone had broken in and opened all the hutch doors and the cage doors. What happened next is rather hazy. We obviously reported it and were given time to sort the animals out and put them back in their cages. At that time we got away lightly. No harm appeared to have been done. But there were consequences. About three to four weeks later, one of my mice gave birth to seven babies. At least I now knew that I had a male and a female!

A couple of weeks after that one of Ann's rabbits had six babies. We knew that both of Ann's rabbits were female, and therefore it was obvious that Floppy was now a father.

We kept small animals throughout the time we attended that school, and in fact in our last year at school, facilities for keeping pets had expanded greatly and had become an important part of the school.

Many years later a brand-new school was built at Hummersknot in Darlington, which we discovered had created a special department to carry on the tradition. We never dreamt when we started off as two third formers with two pet rabbits, that it would develop into such a project.

One of the things that I was really interested in whilst at school was drama. I was happy to take part in anything that was going, even if it was in French. I remember one small part I had in a short dramatic production our French teacher organised. I managed to learn all the lines, and was congratulated later on a flawless performance, which was obviously a miracle as I did not understand one word I was saying!

One year the school put on an outdoor performance of William Shakespeare's *The Tempest*. After auditions I was surprised, but delighted, to be given the part of Stefano, the drunken butler. One of my friends, Judy, played the part of Ariel and some of the scenes were between the two of us. Judy was often suspended from a tree whilst I staggered drunkenly around below her. We gave numerous performances, first to the school and then evening and weekend performances to parents and friends. My mother obviously came to see the show and I remember her telling me how much she had enjoyed it and how proud she was of my performance. However, she wondered how I was able to portray a drunken man so convincingly! I think my success was down to a comedy film I had seen at the cinema. In it, a very wealthy and somewhat posh character slurred his words and walked very unsteadily... I think I simply copied him.

I remember one scene between myself and Ariel when we happened to make eye contact. She was above me on the branch of a tree and I was looking up at her. She and I, like most of my friends at that time, were prone to fits of giggling, and this particular moment was no exception. I don't know how long it was that we remained in limbo, bodies shaking uncontrollably, desperately trying to regain our composure, but I can remember it to this day.

The following year, or maybe it was the year after, the school decided to put on a production of *Noah*. As in previous years we auditioned for parts and I was given the part of Japheth, son of Noah. I was delighted. It was then decided that this particular year the school would bring in a director from outside. The director arrived and re-auditioned us.

Perhaps I should explain the make-up of the school. Most of us were there on merit because we had successfully passed what was then known as the eleven-plus. Of those a percentage were from state schools and the rest from private schools. There were also pupils who had come straight into the school from preparatory school. Having been paying pupils at the preparatory school, these girls did not need to take an examination. One of these girls was my friend Judy. Judy came from a very wealthy family.

All girls mixed well together, though I suppose it was only to be expected that the girls from similar backgrounds became close friends.

My best friends were Ann, whose father was a policeman, Elizabeth (Betty), now known as Liz, whose father was an undertaker and Sheila, who moved to the school from Kings Lynn, in the fourth year.

But back to the point. In many cases those of us who gained a place at that school had accents, whereas many from private schools or preparatory school spoke very well. Most came from very wealthy homes.

When the results of the re-auditioning were announced it was apparent that those of us who had any hint of a Darlington accent were dropped. Hence I no longer had the part of Japheth.

Strangely enough I was then given another part. My gym teacher had been asked to give the names of any pupils who excelled in the gymnasium to act as specific animals. I never gained top marks in French or mathematics, but I was blessed with the ability to balance on a beam or to shin up a rope.

I ended up with the part of a tiger. Strangely enough, even though she had not gained a part in the first auditions, Judy ended up as the monkey. We both enjoyed showing off our acrobatic abilities on stage, though knowing how we were prone to fits of giggles, I think they took a risk when they put us on the stage together once more.

My friend Liz, who we called Betty when we were at school, was crazy about horses. Her love of horses has lasted throughout her life. In her fifties she took early retirement from teaching and set up home in North Wales where she ended up as the proud owner of eight beautiful horses.

As a young girl she spent as much time as she possibly could around horses. One day we cycled out to a nearby farm. Betty had told me that we were going to ride horses that day. I remember feeling extremely nervous as we approached the stables and saw these magnificent animals, heads looking out over the stable doors, snorting and impatiently pawing the ground. They were huge!

However, these were not the horses we were going to ride.

We carried on past the stables until we reached a field. In the field were two horses. One was a rather smart chestnut horse with a flowing mane and tail. She was not as big as the horses in the stable and was obviously quite old. The other one was much smaller, a little bit like one of Thelwell's cartoon ponies. I think she was called Topsy.

The farmer had given Liz permission to ride either one of these two horses providing she brought her own tack. On the back of her bicycle she had strapped two large blankets, and from a small haversack which she carried on her back, she pulled out two lengths of rope. These were to be used as reins. She had one or two other bits and pieces and I watched as she very skilfully attached bits and pieces to the rope and ended up with a homemade bridle and reins. I was then handed one of the blankets and told to copy what she did.

I did as I was told and eventually, having successfully placed the blanket on the horse, with great difficulty, I managed to climb onto the back of Topsy. I seem to remember that Topsy was not very happy.

Eventually we were all ready for me to have my first riding lesson. We started off by walking round the field and then we began to trot. An extremely uncomfortable experience with just a blanket. Towards one end of the field ran a little stream. It flowed diagonally cutting off one corner of the field. In that corner of the field we could see clusters of ripe juicy blackberries. Liz decided that we ought to enjoy eating some of those blackberries…

She also decided that we would jump the stream in order to do so. I was told to copy exactly what she did. She set off racing down the field. Her horse cleared the stream in one leap and she turned and shouted to me to follow. I remember I must have done something right because Topsy set off at what seemed like breakneck speed. I don't think she fancied being left behind with me!

However, on reaching the stream she changed her mind, stopped dead and appeared to lower her head. I carried on, straight over the top of her head, and landed in the stream. I remember it was quite painful, and wet, but probably more embarrassing. I'm sure that when I looked up at Topsy she was looking down at me and grinning!

12

My mother always dressed me in the nicest clothes she could possibly afford. Friends and neighbours would often compliment me and say how much they liked my new dress... jumper... skirt... All so different from the humiliating years at Richmond when children did not want to sit next to me because my clothes had not been washed.

I still remember certain things she bought me. I remember a beautiful bright blue dirndl skirt and a crisp white cotton blouse embroidered with pink rosebuds. But most of all I remember a very special coat.

A new fashion was sweeping the country. It was called the New Look launched by Dior.

The coat my mother bought me was my pride and joy. If ever in my life I have felt like 'a million dollars' it was then! It was dark green in colour and mid-calf in length. It fitted snugly around the neck and the collar was large, curved, and covered the shoulders. The waist fitted tightly, and below that, the skirt was voluminous and long. The buttons were beautiful, shiny and brown. The look was completed by a soft, brown velvet, floppy bow fixed next to the top button. What a pity that my common sense did not match my mother's excellent dress sense.

On one occasion in my early teens, a boy named Ken asked me to go to the pictures with him (back then going to see a film was referred to as a trip to the pictures, not a trip to the cinema as it is today). Ken was a couple of years older than me and compared to me his family were very wealthy. For some reason that I cannot remember, I did not want to tell my mother where I was going. Possibly I was afraid she would not approve of me going to the pictures with a boy. After all it was the first time I had done so, therefore I arranged to meet him a short distance away from my house.

Back then my mother used to wear a cream trench coat to and from work. She also wore a headscarf, quite popular in those days. I remember I always thought she looked very smart. I have no idea what I was thinking at the time, possibly I thought it would make me look older and more grown-up, but I asked her if I could borrow her raincoat and one of her headscarves.

Unaware that I was going on a first 'date', she agreed to let me borrow them. Looking back I can't imagine how horrified Ken must have been when I turned up looking like my mother. We went to the cinema but for some strange reason he never asked me out again! In fact I'm not sure he spoke to me after that. I suppose this recollection is a good time to talk about boyfriends.

As a child I was perfectly happy in my own company, and being solitary was never a problem. However, I valued my friends and enjoyed playing with the boys that I knew.

After all they were always game to do things like climbing trees, and wading in the Beck.

The section of the Dene where the swings were was well used by very young teenagers as a meeting place. We were still young enough to enjoy using the equipment provided, but we also spent a lot of time sitting around and talking.

The Dene was surrounded by tall metal railings and a grassy bank sloped down from the railings to the swings. At one point in the railings, two or three of the uprights had broken away and disappeared. This made a shortcut through the gap and down the grassy bank to the swing park. Two boys, Walter and Ian, were often seen leaning on the top rail and looking down into the park. They were possibly a year older than myself and my friends and very much admired by many of the girls in our group. Walter had blond hair and a lovely smile. lan had dark hair and was the taller of the two. Walter went to the boys' grammar school and Ian attended the local secondary school.

One day I was sitting on one of the swings with Brenda and Stella sitting either side of me on the swings, chatting. Suddenly, a voice said: "Hold on," and my swing was pulled back high into the air and pushed. All I could do was to hang on tightly until eventually the person pushing the swing stopped and slowly brought me to a halt. Then and only then was I able to see who was responsible. I turned to see this boy, with a mop of blond hair and a cheeky grin. I can't remember the exact conversation we had, but it ended up with me agreeing to go for a walk with him. As we walked off I didn't realise at that time that I was the envy of almost every girl in the park.

We talked a lot during that walk. I learned that he lived with his father and that his mother had died when he was very young. After that wherever I went, Walter was there. If

I went on a bike ride he would join me on his bike. He even used to join me when I went to feed the rabbits at school during the long summer holidays.

The exact details of our friendship are quite hazy but I do remember that I grew taller and he didn't. To be quite honest I cannot remember what happened to our friendship. I can't really say he was my first boyfriend as I don't think we ever even held hands. I was probably about thirteen years old.

13

Several of the memories I have related are possibly in the wrong order by quite a few years. I have simply relayed them as they came into my mind.

I vividly remember times spent with Ann. She and I had a very special friendship, a friendship which lasted for a lifetime. Often many years passed without us having the opportunity to meet, but when we did it was as though we had never been apart. The thing I remember most about our meetings was the laughter. At school we were often in trouble for dissolving into fits of laughter, and that never left us, the laughter I mean.

One day, not long after I celebrated my sixtieth birthday, when we were living in Liverton, I had a phone call from Ann. We talked for a long, long time, and yes we laughed for most of it. Ann told me that she had not been well, that she had to use a wheelchair and have immediate access to oxygen. She also said not to worry, she had adapted to it and otherwise she was fine.

We reminisced about the many hilarious escapades we had in our youth, and I felt deliriously happy when I hung up as I always did after spending time with Ann. About a week later I received one of the worst phone calls of my life. One of Ann's daughters rang me to tell me that her mother had died. It was only then that I realised that Ann had called me to say goodbye.

I still get emotional when I think about it, and as I am writing this the tears are very close. But back to happier days.

At the end of the war Ann and her family moved into a flat above the police station. She lived there with her mother, her sister Margaret and her father who (as previously mentioned) was a police sergeant.

Her mother was lovely, always kind and welcoming. Her sister, quite a few years older, looked upon Ann and I as little pests who had been put on this earth to make her life difficult. Her father, a very tall stern-looking man, was actually a very kind and caring man with a great sense of humour. Many of the antics we got up to resulted in a few stern words from her father, but always ended with a shake of the head and a wry smile.

At one time we were members of the Girl Guides. We enjoyed many hours of pure pleasure week after week as we strived to attain more and more proficiency badges. Most of the badges were easy to come by and we were proud of our achievements. However, one badge seemed to elude me. It was the badge for semaphore. I think I failed it on more than one occasion. I remember I caused great hilarity when I was trying to send a message. The two senior guides judging me dissolved into fits of laughter. To this day I don't know what the message was that I sent to them. All I was told was that it was quite rude!

One activity that takes pride of place in my memory is the time when we had a jumble sale. All guides were asked to donate items to help raise funds for a local charity. My mother searched around and found one or two items for me to take to the jumble sale. Probably items that we really needed ourselves, but this was for charity and people helped. She also gave me my bus fare and sixpence to spend.

Ann and I caught the bus to the venue, handed in our donations, helped to set up all the stalls and served behind them until the end of the sale. At the end of the sale we were allowed to look around to see if we spotted anything we would like to buy.

There was not an awful lot left and eventually the things that were left were all put onto one table whilst they started folding up the trestle tables and clearing the hall. Ann and I were offered everything that was left on that table for sixpence. We thought that was an absolute bargain so we bought the lot! My share included a set of metal enamelled pans, two of which had holes in the bottom, all tied together with a piece of string threaded through holes at the end of each handle. I also had a bag full of odds and ends including a teddy bear with one eye. The pièce de résistance was a huge picture in a wooden frame. Cracked glass covered a picture of sand dunes in a desert with one tiny camel only visible if you looked very carefully. The frame was so big that it was very difficult to carry, especially with a set of large pans and a bag of junk.

Ann had even more to carry than I did. Her collection included a huge horn from a gramophone and numerous items that I can't even remember. So picture the scene… two girls in Girl Guide uniforms standing at the bus stop.

One holding a huge gramophone horn which was almost bigger than her and a bag of junk. The other carrying a set of old pans tied together with string, a bag of bits and pieces, with a one-eyed teddy bear peeping from it, and trying to hold on to a very large picture frame with cracked glass.

The bus arrived and, surprise, surprise the bus conductor refused to let us get on the bus. The next bus, and the one after that, also refused to let us get on the bus.

I think we had almost given up hope when the next bus arrived, and after us pleading our case and one or two of the passengers asking the bus conductor to take pity on us, Ann, myself and all our junk were allowed to board the bus.

When we got off the bus Ann talked me into going home with her. I think she thought there was safety in numbers and that her parents would not be too cross if she had a friend with her. It was only on my long solitary walk home struggling to carry everything I had acquired that I realised that I would have nobody to back me up when I eventually reached home and showed my mother what I had bought! I remember she was far from pleased!

A few years later Ann's sister Margaret started university at Durham. Ann and I were by now in our early teens. At a guess about thirteen. Ann and I were sent to visit Margaret in order to deliver certain things from home, including cakes specially made for her by her mum. These gifts were packed into a brand-new leather holdall. We were asked to take special care of the holdall.

However, we carried it between us one handle each and swung it to and fro. One of the handles eventually snapped. I can't remember what we did next, but we ended up with the other handle also breaking. Of course we just thought it was terribly funny.

To Margaret's horror we stayed for a while before starting the long journey home. When we arrived home the enormity of what we had done to the bag hit Ann like a ton of bricks. Once again I agreed to go home with Ann as backup.

As I recall when we arrived at Ann's home, we opened the door just enough to push the bag in first using a broomstick and waited for a reaction. I remember that her mother was very angry and we both received a good telling-off. However, that was nothing to the telling-off we had after Ann's parents received a letter from Margaret asking her mother never to send Ann and her friend to visit her again. She claimed that our visit was both embarrassing and humiliating.

Around about the same time a new pupil joined our school. Her name was Sheila. She and her family had moved from Kings Lynn to Darlington. Sheila joined my form and she and I became firm friends, almost inseparable, until the day I left to go to college.

14

I have always had a love of the great outdoors. I think the years in Richmond when alone as a child spending so many happy hours exploring woodland, meadows and riverbanks was the beginning of that love.

My friendship with Sheila was the start of many years of exploration and discovery, initially on the Yorkshire Moors and in the Yorkshire Dales and eventually further afield with us actually reaching the Isle of Arran.

Sheila and I started off with long hikes, usually undertaken at the weekend. We would start early in the morning taking with us a rucksack containing lunch and something waterproof. Quite often we were joined by Betty (Liz) and by Molly.

Molly also came to the school when her parents moved into the area. She also became part of a group which by now included myself and friends Ann, Betty (now known as Liz) Sheila, Marjorie and Molly. Molly was very different to the rest of us. Her parents were extremely wealthy. She was used to the finer things in life and often found it difficult to join in with some of the activities if it meant there was a possibility of her ending up with muddy shoes or dirty hands! A little bit like the character Penelope Keith played in the sitcom *The Good Life*.

I'll never forget the first day we were allowed to visit her at her house. Ann, Liz and I took a bus to a village just outside Darlington, followed the instructions she had given us and eventually found her house. Two huge iron gates opened onto a drive which led to the front door. The door was answered by a young lady, never did we find out who she was, and we stepped into a large hallway. I think I stood there with my mouth open for quite some time as I took in the view. In front of me, a wide staircase led up to a galleried landing which stretched around all four sides of the hall. Off the galleried landing were doors obviously leading to bedrooms, bathrooms etc. I had never seen anything like it other than in films. I had no idea that ordinary people could live in such luxury!

But back to the point, the four of us enjoyed many days out, especially in the long summer holidays.

One day the geography department at school organised a weekend visit to the moors in higher Teesdale. We stayed at the youth hostel in Langdon Beck. This was our first experience of youth hostels and we loved it. We enjoyed every minute of it, and everything worked like clockwork until the moment we were due to leave.

Buses had arrived to take us home but there was one girl missing. Initially this caused a panic until somebody spotted her walking back towards the hostel across a field.

The previous day, on our way to visit the spectacular High Force – an impressive waterfall on the river Tees – we had explored nearby rocky outcrops. The teacher described in detail the kind of rocks that we could see, one of which was basalt. Back at the hostel later that day she pointed to a rocky outcrop we could see in the distance. She explained that many of the same kind of rocks, including basalt, could be found there.

The girl who had caused all the panic eventually arrived back at the hostel, collected her things and boarded the bus. We discovered later that she had misheard the word 'basalt'. She thought the teacher had said bath salt and had walked across the fields to bring some back as a gift. I can't remember the girl's name, but I don't think she ever lived that down. Everybody always connected her to bath salts!

After the initial introduction to youth hostels, Sheila and I decided to join the Association. We also equipped ourselves with the necessary attire. Sheila's parents were quite rich so she ended up with extremely good-quality equipment. Most of my equipment came from the local army and navy stores.

I was equipped with shorts and trousers (trousers were new to me and up till then I had only ever worn skirts or shorts). I had a new waterproof jacket and a huge khaki army surplus oilskin cape and sou'wester hat. My rucksack was enormous, also army surplus. How soldiers carried them, full of all their heavy equipment, I'll never know. They were actually heavy before you put anything in them, partly due to the metal frame on the back. At the bottom of the rucksack the metal frame curved to fit around your waist and sit comfortably on your hips. Actually comfortably is the wrong word to use. The last things to be purchased were a pair of boots and some thick socks, again army surplus.

Most weekends hail, rain or shine, Sheila and I would set off to walk well-trodden and popular routes, always ending up at a youth hostel where we spent the night.

We met many people on our trips. People from all walks of life and people from other countries. I remember one night in particular when we were sharing a dormitory with some girls from Holland. They were on a school trip and their English was perfect. Suddenly our dormitory was invaded by six boys in their group. We sat and talked until the early hours. One of the boys, his name was Fritz, sat on my bed. We learned a lot that night, especially about life in Holland during the war. We made new friends. That was one of the wonderful things about youth hostels… new friends and new experiences each time.

The following day their school party departed for pastures new and we set off for home. We had great memories and made new friends, and I think that for the first time in my life I had fallen a little bit in love. Perhaps that is why as we walked across the moors, we sang very loudly a popular song of the time 'Bewitched, Bothered and Bewildered'.

On one occasion Sheila and I had been walking in the Cleveland Hills. We were heading for a little village called Lastingham, to the youth hostel there. It had been a long day of walking and we were exhausted when we reached Lastingham. To our horror the youth hostel was closed. We had no idea what to do. There were no buses to take us further on, and we were certainly too tired to walk. The only option was to try to find accommodation in Lastingham.

There was only one choice, the local pub! Neither Sheila nor myself had ever been inside a pub, let alone stayed in one, but we plucked up the courage to go inside. Feeling very, very nervous, we approached the bar and asked the lady standing behind it whether or not we could stay there for the night.

I will never forget the kindness we received that night. We were taken upstairs to a lovely bedroom where we found the most comfortable bed with crisp white sheets and fluffy pillows.

Later, we were served supper. We sat in the corner of the bar and enjoyed hot soup and a hot drink. The locals were very friendly and wanted to know all about our walk. The following morning the landlord served us a hearty breakfast.

When we attempted to pay he asked us how much we would have paid in the hostel. He refused to take one penny more. At a guess the year was about 1948 and we were fourteen years old.

15

Over the next couple of years, Sheila and I explored most of the Dales, much of the Yorkshire Moors and ventured as far as the Lake District.

We stayed in places like Kirby Stephen, Kirby Moorside, Malham, Saltburn-by-the-Sea, Robin Hood's Bay, Penrith, Askrigg, Aysgarth Falls, Barnard Castle, Sedbergh, Stainforth, Wolsingham, and many more.

Eventually we reached an age where we needed to concentrate much more on our education. Also friendships with boys took on a new meaning. Gone were the days of the tomboy able to keep up with any boy climbing a tree or catching the most tadpoles.

Now it was a case of making sure that we combed our hair and looked presentable before we left school.

If I remember rightly, co-educational secondary schools did not become the norm in the UK until the '70s. Back in the '40s and '50s all forms of secondary education were single sex.

In Darlington the boys' grammar school and the girls' grammar school were situated in the same area of town. The location of the girls' grammar school, known as Darlington

High School for Girls, meant that going to and from school, we all had to walk past the boys' grammar school, known as Queen Elizabeth's Grammar School for Boys.

When I was in the fifth form I remember our school changed the times of our afternoon session. We started earlier in the afternoon, meaning that we shaved half an hour off lunchtime and therefore finished school half an hour earlier. It was meant to ensure that we were all safely on our way home before the boys came out of school. This gave the senior girls plenty of time to comb their hair and make sure they looked at their best before setting off!

We were growing up. We were becoming teenagers. We had new interests and followed new pursuits.

I became interested in roller skating. The South Park in Darlington was where most people who wanted to skate congregated. Next to the bandstand was a skating rink, where beginners and experienced skaters skated together. The rink was built around the bandstand where sometimes music played. Around one side of the rink a bank dotted with trees sloped upwards.

The bank was home to many benches, put there so that people could sit and listen to the music and watch the skaters. It was also a place to meet friends.

Skating did not come easy to me. I think that was mostly down to the fact that the kind of roller skates most of us owned were the kind that were adjustable in size, and clamped to the soles of your shoes. Just as you reached an acceptable speed, one of the clips would come loose and the skate would leave your shoe, though still be attached to your ankle by a strap, and down you would go. Extremely unflattering, embarrassing and often very painful.

Of course experienced skaters had spent money purchasing boots with wheels attached.

Many years later, possibly in the '70s, I used to envy those who owned roller boots. They appeared to be so much smoother and were definitely quieter than our old roller skates!

I also enjoyed trying (note the word trying!) to play tennis. Stanhope Park, North Lodge Park and South Park all had tennis courts. I was given a tennis racket – I think from my godmother – which she no longer needed. I remember it came with a wooden press in the shape of an isosceles trapezium. Two identical pieces were placed on either side of the racket and screwed tightly together with butterfly thumb screws. It certainly helped to keep the racket in good shape but made it very heavy to carry. Once again a pastime I enjoyed, but I'm afraid I was not very proficient.

I had no difficulty in hitting the ball over the net, the problem was it was usually the netting fence which surrounded the tennis court! Sport was not my forte. I enjoyed netball and became reasonably proficient, but hockey and tennis not so good. I actually hated hockey! I could never see the point of racing up and down a waterlogged hockey pitch on a cold, often rainy, day, to end up having your shins whacked with a stick.

However, one thing in which I did excel was gymnastics. I could shin up a rope, balance on a beam and use a springboard to successfully clear the vaulting horse or the pommel horse in various acrobatic ways.

Each year at school we had prize-giving day. Prizes were given to all pupils who had achieved exceptional results in a variety of subjects. When it came to outstanding achievements in sport, 'colours' were presented.

Each year I climbed the steps to the platform to receive my colours for gymnastics. I don't think I have ever felt such elation!

Another pastime I enjoyed in those early teenage years was dancing. I attended various groups at different venues in the town. Country dancing was one such group. I really enjoyed this group. I think my favourite dance of all was the lancers. I always had the same partner for this particular dance. He was a soldier, extremely tall as I remember. This particular dance involves lots of extremely fast swinging in circles. My feet never touched the ground because my partner was so tall.

I also joined a group of square dancers.

16

My visits to Richmond on Saturday mornings became more regular. I began to worry about my grandmother coping on her own. I worried about her being alone in the flat that I had once shared with her.

I must have conveyed these feelings to my mother each week, and therefore feel responsible for the fact that my mother felt it was her duty to take care of my grandmother.

Why should I say I feel responsible? That infers that it was not a good thing that I did. At the time I didn't realise that. At the time I just thought it would be great for us all to live together safely.

At the time I never gave a thought to the fact that my mother was already struggling to look after me, to let me have the education that she was denied. It's only in later years when we look back that we realise what life was like for other people.

I can't remember the exact year, but sometime in my early teens, my mother managed to get a mortgage on number 37 Greenbank Road, Darlington. It was a beautiful house. It had four bedrooms, a huge attic, a large front sitting room, a dining room, a cosy kitchen, a scullery, a huge larder and so much more.

We all moved in, I had my own bedroom at the front of the house. My grandmother had a bedroom at the top of the stairs next to the toilet and bathroom, and had her own room downstairs, a large room which was originally the dining room.

For the first time, since the time we had to leave number 19 Parkside because of the outbreak of the war, we enjoyed the luxury of an indoor toilet and a bath which could be instantly filled with hot water!

I loved that house. I never tired of the space and loved to spend time in the attic. A door on the upper landing led to a staircase which in turn led to the attic. It was a huge room. The floor space covered the same space as three bedrooms, two at the front and one at the back. We used it as a storage room and over the years more and more things were stored up there. When I was up there I also loved to stand on tiptoe and peer out through the skylights in the roof. I felt I could see for miles across the rooftops. Not so many years ago I paid a nostalgic visit to Darlington, drove round and looked at all the places that I remembered. I noticed that number 37 Greenbank Road now had dormer windows in the loft and I can only imagine what it looks like inside now.

17

In the summer of 1950 I had my sixteenth birthday and like a lot of my friends this opened new avenues of entertainment. At sixteen we were allowed to attend a venue in town called Palais de Dance. The venue was a huge hall with a raised platform at one end where a dance band played for the evening. Chairs were placed down both sides of the hall.

Back in the early '50s, in towns all across the country, this was the place that many people went to meet friends, to meet boys or girls and to dance. Life has changed so much since then. It was almost unheard of for young people to frequent pubs and bars. Instead we met in coffee bars. The most popular coffee bar in Darlington was called The Green Tree. This was where we often met, a place where a cup of tea or an ice cream would usually last all night. When we reached sixteen and were able to go to an organised dance, it was exciting. The evening usually started off with all the girls sitting down one side, all the boys sitting down the other side of the room, and the boys who thought they were the John Travoltas of the group, used to stand in groups near the entrance door.

When the band started to play, boys – hesitant at first – would venture across the room to ask a girl for a dance, and it wasn't long before the dance floor was filled with couples dancing. Some were good, some were hopeless, and some just danced on the spot. I was usually one of the lucky ones and I danced most of the night.

I remember one night in particular. It was the beginning of the spring term 1951.

A group of young trainee pilots had come in from Middleton St George. Middleton St George was used during World War Two as an air base and just after the war it alternated between Bomber Command, Fighter Command and Flying Training Command. I remember going weak at the knees when a particularly good-looking young man/boy came to ask me for a dance. His name was Gordon. We got on really well. It turned out he was the youngest of the group. They were training to fly jet engines.

Most of them were in their early twenties but he was barely eighteen. I remember we danced all night and then he walked me home. It was then that he asked if he could see me again the following week. It goes without saying that I said yes and thus began a friendship.

He was quiet, quite reserved and didn't want to get involved in the escapades that some of his older, more experienced colleagues got up to every week. Our friendship gave him an excuse – he had a girlfriend!

I was quite happy to go along with it; I enjoyed his company, he wasn't a bad dancer, he was easy on the eye, and there was a certain kudos about going out with a guy in uniform. Also on one occasion he flew very low across our school and it felt great to know that it was for me! I was the envy of the fifth form!

However, all good things must come to an end. When I first started meeting him I knew that the unit he was in were only there for a short period of training time and that they would be moved without notice to another base at any time.

Eventually that time came. It was expected, but I missed our Saturday nights at the Palais. Fortunately Sheila and I had a holiday planned. So I didn't have time to mope.

18

One holiday that will always stand out in my memory is when Sheila and I travelled to Scotland and visited Loch Lomond and the Isle of Arran. If my memory serves me correctly, we broke up for the summer holidays quite early that year. The year was 1951. The first year of O levels. We had all worked hard and were apprehensively awaiting the results. Some of us were more apprehensive than others.

Sheila and I had already planned to go on a youth hostelling holiday, so on the last day of term we were already packed and ready. We left home early. At that time we had no particular plans just that this was going to be a holiday with a difference. Something to remember for a long time. And it certainly was.

We headed to the bus station where we already had tickets as far as Carlisle. I have a photograph taken at the bus station in Carlisle.

I can't really remember where we got to on the first day, but I have a feeling that we arrived in Girvan and stayed in a hostel nearby. The following day we boarded the ferry at Ardrossan and sailed across to the Isle of Arran.

I will never forget the island, its beauty and the friendliness of the people.

We spent quite a few days on the island and stayed at both hostels Brodick and Lochranza. During our time there we explored as much of the island as we were able to.

One of the wonderful things about youth hostelling was meeting other people. People from all walks of life. People from all parts of our country, England, Scotland, Wales and Ireland. People from all parts of Europe. People from all over the world. People of different ethnicities and backgrounds.

One of the most exciting days was the day we climbed Goat Fell. We were able to leave our huge rucksacks at the hostel and so were able to enjoy the day unencumbered. During the holiday I learned many things. I learned what a beautiful place this world is, though to be honest I already knew that from my exploration of the Yorkshire Moors and the Dales. I also learned that the world is a very small place.

Sheila and I had begun cooking our meal in the kitchen of the hostel on our very first evening there, and suddenly a voice behind us said, "What are you two doing here?" We turned to see two friends from school, Joan and Elizabeth, who were twins. They were in our class at school and they were the last people we expected to see. It still seems incredible that the four of us had ended up in exactly the same place, at exactly the same time.

However, the following day we decided to climb Goat Fell together.

That was a day to be remembered – I remember clear blue skies and lots of sunshine. A beautiful day to enjoy the freedom of the hills. We were joined along the way by three boys we had already met at the hostel. I think their names were Spud (obviously a nickname) Tom and Keith. At least that is what I've written on the photograph we took.

Halfway along the walk we came across the remains of a small light aircraft which had obviously crashed on the island at some time. We climbed all over it and took photographs. We imagined that it possibly had something to do with the war which after all was only six years in the past. To reach the summit we had to climb through the clouds, and I still remember the feeling of exhilaration as we eventually climbed above them and reached the peak of Goat Fell. We have a photograph taken at the summit.

Photographs back then were taken with a brownie box camera so every single one is precious.

We parted company with Elizabeth and Joan after a couple of days. I think they were moving on to somewhere else. I do know that they became great friends with two of the boys that we met at the hostel. In fact one of the twins ended up marrying one of the boys. I can't remember which twin and I can't remember which boy, but the last time I heard (which is one heck of a long time ago) they were still married.

The day we climbed Chir Mior we set off, just the two of us, in great excitement with wonderful expectations of the day ahead. It wasn't long before we were joined by a couple of teenage boys from Leeds. I remember them as if it were yesterday – Oliver and Neville. I don't think I had ever heard such strong Yorkshire accents as they had. I was fascinated and remember that I just wanted them to keep talking so that I could listen. We ended up walking in twos.

Sheila walked with Oliver and I walked with Neville. I had to keep asking him to repeat things as his accent was so strong I could barely understand what he was saying. I remember he told me he worked in a treacle factory, making Pudsey treacle. It sounded absolutely horrendous and I could understand his joy at being out in the open enjoying fresh air and open countryside. I enjoyed his company for the rest of the day. That evening everybody met up in the common room after supper and a very enjoyable evening was spent meeting new people, exchanging stories and just enjoying one another's company. The following day we waved goodbye and I don't think I ever thought about him again until now as I am writing this.

I say this because as we go through life we meet so many people who touch our lives so briefly. It is only now as I recall those early carefree days that I wonder what happened to him. What did he do with his life? Did he have a good life? Is he still alive? I'll never know.

Sheila and I spent quite a few days exploring the rest of the island including Lochranza. Then came the sad day when we had to leave.

Some days in life are etched in one's memory. And the day we left the Isle of Arran will always stay in my memory. As the ferry pulled away from the harbour, a pipe band played, 'Will ye no come back again?', and at that moment I felt that I would come back again. Sadly I have never managed to do so. After the Isle of Arran we travelled up to Loch Lomond. I don't think we took buses. Instead we thumbed a lift in various trucks and lorries – something we had promised our parents we would not do. I would certainly not advocate doing it in this day and age, but back then it seemed perfectly safe.

The hostel at Loch Lomond was very different from any we had stayed in before. It was huge, more like a castle. I remember it for two very different reasons. The main reason is because that was where I met Wally, whom I will speak about later.

The second reason is one I would really rather forget, but one I have never been able to forget for the whole of my life. Each evening in the hostel they had concerts or dancing in the main hall. At one end of the hall was a raised platform, and when we were there a group of musicians played to entertain the many people who were staying in the hostel.

People who came from all over the world, from different nationalities and different religions. It was a wonderful time to be able to meet all these people, to talk to them, to understand them and to make new friends. At the end of the evening the band who had been playing all evening said that to close the evening they would like to welcome people from all over the world. They did this by asking people from various countries to stand up and to clap and cheer those people.

One by one different countries were asked to take the floor, including France, Belgium, Holland, America, Ireland and Wales to name a few. Each time the band applauded and cheered and welcomed the people from those countries to Scotland, Sheila and I joined in. At that moment it was a happy place, but that was to change. Eventually, right at the end, the band asked people from England to stand. There were three of us who stood up that night back in 1951. Two sixteen-year-old girls and one equally young boy who, up until that moment, had been so happy to be in such a beautiful country full of what we thought were beautiful people.

What followed was like a nightmare. The claps and cheers which began from the rest of the audience were drowned out by boos from the band and the Scottish staff who were in the audience. The booing continued until three traumatised young people left the hall.

I think we were comforted by people from other countries who really couldn't understand what was going on. I think that was the first time in my life where I had felt pure hatred directed towards me and my friends, and the most dreadful part of it was I didn't know why!

The following morning we decided to leave Scotland. Fortunately this happened at the end of our holiday and not at the beginning. It took many years before my husband Derek helped me to rebuild a love for that country.

19

However, besides the wonderful memories I had of the Isle of Arran and its people, I also met another very, very good friend on the day I was leaving. His name was Wally. He was Belgian and for some reason he singled me out from the crowd. We talked for a long time. He took photographs, we exchanged addresses and then he called to see me on his way back down to Dover. He ended up staying for a week or more and we had a wonderful time together.

We corresponded over the next year and he came to England once more to stay with us. I know he actually asked my mother if he could take me back to Belgium with him. I know he hoped for a lot more from the friendship than I was able to give. I liked him as a friend, but that was all. We did have good times together whilst he was staying with us. He was happy. He learned to laugh again.

I remember one occasion when we visited Durham. We had explored the cathedral and the surrounding streets and decided to take canoes out on the river. We were doing quite well; I was ahead chattering away fifty to the dozen as I usually did, and had rounded a bend in the river, when I realised nobody was answering me. I slowed up and turned around to find Wally was nowhere to be seen. I immediately turned around and made my way back. As I rounded the bend in the river I saw him. He was no longer sitting in the canoe, instead he was standing, trousers rolled up, up to his knees in water trying desperately to dislodge his canoe from the sandbank he had ended up on!

I am afraid I laughed. If something looks funny I can't help it. I've been like that all my life. I laughed till the tears rolled down my cheeks and eventually Wally laughed too. I remember how good it was to see him laugh. He and my mother corresponded for a long time after that. Since she died I have found many letters that he sent to her. He always loved coming to stay with us. He said it was the one place where he found laughter. He told us that his family did not laugh anymore. Reading between the lines I think they had had a pretty rough time during the war.

One of the last letters he wrote to my mother was to say that he was soon to be called up to do his national service. There the letters ended and I don't know what happened to him. In recent years with technology now available I have tried to trace him, but sadly have been unable to do so.

I loved the holiday we had on the Isle of Arran.

I have enjoyed many holidays in Scotland since with Derek, with John and Tim, with friends, and I love Scotland. Strangely I have never been back to Loch Lomond. I have no wish to do so.

It is quite amazing how two days from the same holiday still remain so vividly in my mind.

One displaying the genuine friendship of the people of the Isle of Arran as the sound of the pipes travelled across the sea asking us to return.

The other… I only wish I could forget!

20

The next bit of excitement in 1951 was the day we went to school to receive the results of our O levels. Nobody knew what to expect. O levels were in their first year. I felt reasonably confident, not that I would achieve great things but that I would pass.

Maths was my big worry. I think it was my maths teacher's worry as well. If my memory serves me correctly her name was Miss Lax.

We were each called into the headteacher's study where we were given our results. I came out walking on air. I had passed everything, even my maths. I remember as I came out of the head's room an excited Miss Lax grabbed hold of me and gave me a hug. She was both delighted and extremely surprised at the same time.

Then it was back to school. Time to decide which A levels we wanted to carry on with. At this point in time I still had no idea what I wanted to do for the future.

Entering the sixth form came with extra responsibilities. Many of us were appointed as prefects. I still remember being called up onto the stage to be introduced to the school and to be presented with my prefect badge.

I remember looking down at the very front rows of girls. Girls who had just started at the school. Most of them were still very nervous and very unsure about their surroundings. I remember looking at them and thinking, *it is not so long ago that I stood where you are, and I cannot believe that I am standing here now as a prefect.* When we first started the school we were allocated to a specific house. There were four houses at Darlington High School for Girls. They were Bede, Caedmon, Hilda and Wycliffe. I was always proud to be part of Caedmon.

Each year someone was elected to be the captain of each house. This was normally a step up having been elected as vice house captain the year before. I was shocked, delighted, surprised and unable to believe that I was elected as vice captain for Caedmon house. After all, this was an election by other pupils.

I was walking on air. I'd passed all my O levels, I was a prefect, I was vice captain of my house with the knowledge that the following year I would be the captain. I couldn't believe it. I couldn't believe that I, Audrey Smith, could achieve anything like that. Things couldn't get better! It all seemed too good to be true!

21

Home life was great. School was great. I even had a new boyfriend, Dave.

Then I started getting pains, especially when I laughed. One night after church I met Dave and we went for a walk. I remember asking him not to make me laugh because it hurt too much. That night was the last time I saw him for many months, because that's when I realised I was really ill. That night I developed a fever.

I can remember my mother rolling me from one blanket into another as I soaked each one with perspiration. Eventually she went next door to ask our neighbours to phone the doctor.

Few people had telephones in those days, unless you needed it for business (our next-door neighbour was a taxi driver) or unless you had lots of money. The doctor, Doctor Woodman, arrived quickly. He immediately arranged for me to be admitted to hospital as an emergency. I was rushed into Darlington Memorial Hospital.

I have no recollection of being taken to hospital, or of the examinations and treatment that went on over the next few days. I have a few hazy memories of being in a bed somewhere in the hospital.

I remember it wasn't a normal ward with beds down both sides. I was lying in a bed, with other patients each side of me, in a long veranda which had the windows open wide at all times.

I found out later that they were worried about tuberculosis (TB). TB was prevalent at that time and it was thought that one of the best ways to treat it was with fresh air. Hence the open veranda.

After a couple of weeks and many tests I was declared not to be suffering from tuberculosis. I was diagnosed with a severe attack of pleurisy. I was then moved to Friarage Hospital in Northallerton, where I was to stay until almost Christmas.

Friarage Hospital was founded in the early years of World War Two and, by 1943, had become an RAF hospital.

When I arrived on the ward in the Friarage, I never dreamed that I would be there till almost Christmas. I occupied a bed in a long ward which I think was one of a series of long wooden huts stretching from the main building.

Life in hospital back then was so different. These days after any illness or surgery you are encouraged to get on your feet as soon as possible. Back then if the doctor ordered bed rest it meant just that. I was not allowed to get out of bed at all, for any reason. Day after day went by following the same routine.

At about 6am or even earlier the nurses who had been on duty overnight would perform their last task, which was to bring round bowls of water for us to have our morning wash. Most of us were long-stay patients and some were still teenagers like me. Next to me was a sixteen-year-old girl named Celia. She had something wrong with her spine. We became good friends.

There was another girl about the same age as us in the bed on the other side of me. We soon got tired of being awakened at such an unearthly hour and the three of us all played the same trick.

Before we went to sleep we would rub a little soap onto a face cloth and leave it within reach on our bedside table. When the water bowls were placed next to us at the crack of dawn we would simply reach out, squeeze the face cloth in the water and then turn over and go back to sleep. The days were long enough. We were quite happy to sleep until breakfast was served which was a couple of hours later.

I'm sure the nurses knew what we were doing and turned a blind eye to it. After breakfast they always brought us water to clean our teeth, and we had a chance to wash our hands and face. Every day was the same. Breakfast, teeth cleaning, hair brushing etc.

Then came bed making. This was a military operation. Sheets were changed regularly and hospital corners had to be immaculate. Each and every bed had to look absolutely pristine, and that meant that the patients in them were almost totally immobilised because sheets and blankets were tucked in so tightly that they could barely breathe, let alone move. The reason for this was the visit of Matron.

Matron ruled that hospital with a rod of iron. Each day she would do her rounds, and visit each and every ward in the hospital. Patients were propped up on their pillows with arms outside the tightly stretched sheets and blankets, whilst Matron walked up one side of the ward and down the other. The ward sister would walk with her and nurses on duty would stand at various points on the ward seemingly holding their breath.

As soon as she left the ward and the inspection was over, life would start again. Those patients who were able to would release themselves from their tight bindings, and those who were too ill to do so would be assisted by the nurses.

Then followed a couple of hours when the sound of a radio programme called *Housewives' Choice* boomed out from loudspeakers placed around the ward. During this time doctors would visit patients around the ward, patients would be given bed baths and other daily routines would take place.

The afternoons allowed visitors, though because Northallerton Friarage Hospital was 'out of town', few of the patients received visitors on weekdays. We all looked forward to the weekend when we would see our loved ones. How I looked forward to weekends. I can't remember the exact time – I think it was probably 1pm – the ward doors were opened and in poured the visitors.

All eyes were fixed on those doors and the feeling of elation when I saw my mother was immense. It was hard for my mother. She still had to work each day. At this time she was working at Darlington Chemical Works, providing tea and refreshments to all the staff at the numerous offices and departments. Everyone loved her. She walked to work each day and then walked home after work. The distance was just under two miles each way. When she got home she had to prepare food for my grandmother and also see to her many needs. As I was to learn years later this was without any gratitude on the part of my grandmother who became very difficult as the years went by.

But on top of all this she found time to bake cakes for me and to make jars of lemon curd which she brought in each week… and oh how I enjoyed them! There is still nothing like my mother's home-made lemon curd!

Weeks went by, and the weeks turned into months. During this time the only time I left my bed was when I was taken by wheelchair to see the doctors, sometimes for X-rays, and sometimes, at the beginning of my stay, for pleural effusions.

I remember the first time I had a pleural effusion. The nurse explained that she was going to put a needle through my ribs and into my lung to remove fluid. She suggested it was better that I didn't look at the syringe. Obviously having been told not to look made me look! She was right I should not have done so! The syringe was the size that you would normally see a vet use on a horse. It was terrifying and yes it was painful. Fortunately as the weeks went on this procedure was abandoned.

However, I consoled myself that my plural effusions were nowhere near as bad as Celia's lumber punctures. Celia had to have these at regular intervals. It was traumatising to hear her scream and beg the nurses not to take her as they were wheeling her out of the ward. She was always heavily sedated when she was brought back and it took a couple of days for her to be her normal self again.

Whilst I was in hospital I had lots of time to think. Time to think about my future. I'd never really thought about it before. Lots of people wrote to me during this time. One of them was Wally, the boy I had met at the hostel in Loch Lomond. He was shocked that I was so ill. I had been so fit and full of life whilst he was staying with us only a few weeks previously. He also sent me the gift of a gold watch. His sister was visiting the UK, so she wore it as she entered the country and then posted it to me. I wore it for many years until it gave up. I still have it and I suppose it could be repaired.

Besides hearing from Wally and other friends, I had a letter from Nessie. I had known her all my life. She was my first friend when we lived at Parkside. She was slightly older than me and was writing to tell me that she had just begun two years at Didsbury College where she was training to be a teacher. She described life at the college and everything sounded wonderful. Because my birthday fell in August I actually was eligible to go to college one whole year before my classmates. The more I thought about it the more enticing it became. I talked to my mother who in turn went to speak to my headmistress, Miss Jewsbury.

To cut a long story short Miss Jewsbury visited me in hospital and we had a long discussion. She then re-visited me with application forms, helped me to complete them and then posted them for me to Didsbury College. Miss Jewsbury included a covering letter explaining my position and the fact that I was in hospital.

Sometime at the beginning of December the doctors obviously decided that I was ready to be allowed out of bed. This was a wonderful day. A day I'd been looking forward to for months, not weeks. Standing up felt strange. I was using muscles that I had not used since September. The worst part of it was the pain in my feet.

I honestly don't think that these days someone would be allowed to lie in bed for that length of time without having to do leg exercises and without something being done to keep the soles of the feet from becoming so soft.

The soles of my feet had become so soft that it felt as though the actual bones were pressing right through them.

Each evening after practising walking up and down the ward, a nurse would come to massage my feet with warm water and soap and then with surgical spirit. This was meant to strengthen the soles of my feet and make them ready for walking again. It was absolute bliss and something I looked forward to every day. It did help but it took a couple of months before I could actually walk without pain.

Eventually the day I had been longing for arrived and it was time to go home. Strangely that particular day was a day of mixed emotions.

On the one hand, I couldn't wait to leave that place and go home to see my own bedroom, my own possessions, see my mother and my friends, and in fact just go back to living a normal life. On the other hand came sudden waves of emotion. A great sadness that I would leave the nurses who looked after me so well, especially one called Nurse Stevenson (we were never allowed to use Christian names). Friends that I had made including the young boys and men in the next ward that we used to wave to through the windows, from whom we used to receive written messages and send our replies. Messages carried by the nurses who were also our friends. They say it does not take long to become institutionalised and I think that is true. The ward and that bed had been my home for a long time. It felt safe. I felt secure there.

However, the longing for home was even stronger and I couldn't wait to get there.

22

It was wonderful to be home but it also felt strange. It was so quiet and I felt myself waiting to be told what to do next. But I soon got used to it and enjoyed every minute of my freedom, at least I did after I had visited the dentist.

I arrived home suffering from horrendous toothache. It had started in the hospital but I was reluctant to say anything in case it delayed my discharge. My mother made an appointment for me to visit the dentist but I remember I had to somehow get through a weekend first. The pain was so bad that it was impossible for me to sleep!

My mother's dear friend Charles Harrison came to the rescue. I have been told many times since that what they tried was simply an old wives' tale. But old wives' tale or not it worked! At that time my grandmother used to enjoy a glass of milk stout with her supper every evening. Back then it was considered to be beneficial to health. After all it was full of iron. I am told that many doctors and hospitals actually prescribed it for their patients.

But back to the old wives' tale. It was said that if a red-hot poker was plunged into stout or Guinness it would most certainly help you to sleep. Thus it was decided that anything was worth trying. The procedure was carried out, the stout was poured into a glass, and I was told to drink it. The pain was so bad at that time that I would have tried anything! It obviously worked. I slept… and slept… and slept.

After which I visited the dentist, my tooth was extracted, and I returned home. I have no recollection of any of it! I do remember though the wonderful feeling of being free from pain.

I have since discovered that 'beer poking' or inserting a hot rod into beer to warm it, is a custom that has been practised for hundreds of years in certain parts of the world. Certainly in Germany and more recently in Texas, USA. However, I suspect that as it was my very first introduction to alcohol of any sort, I would have slept whether or not the red-hot poker had been used!

I remember Christmas was very enjoyable, but very quiet.

I was still finding it difficult to walk very far, as the soles of my feet were still not fully recovered, and it was still extremely painful to stand for long periods.

Friends called to see me, including those who had not managed to get out to the Friarage at Northallerton. It was great to see them all and to catch up with what had been going on whilst I had been in hospital.

One of the people who called was Celia. Celia was discharged from hospital just after Christmas. We both owed the doctors and nurses at the Friarage Hospital a great deal. We were sent to that hospital when we were both very ill, and after months of treatment here we were, fully recovered and ready to face the world. Over the years I lost contact with Celia but I hope she went on to fulfil her dreams, whatever they were.

23

Shortly after I came out of hospital I had a letter from Didsbury College inviting me to go for an interview in January. I can't remember the exact date but I was aware that most interviews had already taken place and that most places had been filled. I felt privileged to have been given an interview.

The next step was to get myself to the interview. There was absolutely no chance of my mother being able to take time from work to go with me. It was something I had to do on my own.

I was a small town girl, unused to the hurly-burly of city life. Yes I had experienced busy stations in London and in Edinburgh, but at that time I was a child and I did not have to think, only follow.

The first part of the journey was relatively easy. I had to take the train from Bank Top Station in Darlington to Manchester. There had always only been one way to get to Bank Top Station in Darlington and that was to walk. I estimated it was about a mile and a half from my house to the station and the second half of the journey was all uphill. I presume that is why the station was originally named Bank Top!

Besides being painful when I walked, if I had been on my feet for any length of time my ankles would swell up like balloons. Hence by the time I reached the station I probably looked a little bit like Michelin Man... at least around my feet.

The journey from Darlington to Manchester was quite uneventful. I eventually stepped out onto the platform. If my memory serves me right the station was Manchester Piccadilly. A wee bit different to Darlington Bank Top Station!

To start with, it was the number of people who all seemed to be in a hurry. The second thing was the noise. Announcements all over the place about trains leaving or arriving. I eventually managed to find my way out of the station.

It was then I realised I had absolutely no idea how I was going to get to Didsbury College. I had obviously been given advice as to what to do, i.e. find a bus going to Didsbury. Not an easy task. There were so many buses! All going to places I'd never heard of.

However, a few enquiries from people who looked approachable enough to speak to, eventually saw me onto the right bus and on my way to Didsbury.

I eventually arrived at my destination. As I stepped down from the bus I don't think I have ever felt so terrified. My ankles were still like balloons, every step felt as though somebody was driving nails through the bottom of my feet, and as I turned to take my first look at Didsbury College I wondered for one moment what on earth I was doing there. The building looked imposing and in front of me was a large gated entrance.

I don't remember much about how I found my way into the building but I have vivid recollections of sitting in a room in front of a large desk, behind which sat the principal, Mr Alfred Body. Sitting either side of Mr Body were two lecturers, Mr Seymour and Mr Seabridge.

All three looked very imposing and were wearing smart suits and full-length black gowns. Somehow I got through the interview (which seemed to go on forever), managed to answer all the questions and at the end of it, to my utter amazement, I was offered a place in the college starting in September 1952.

Later I came to know Mr Seymour and Mr Seabridge very well as they were both English lecturers and English literature was my main subject.

Of course then followed the task of finding my way back to the station, finding the right train, boarding it and travelling back to Darlington.

I don't know how many weeks it took but eventually my feet recovered, my ankles stopped swelling and I was totally back to normal.

24

Then the hard work started. Originally I had intended to work towards A levels in English literature and in art. That would have taken two years. As things stood now I needed to gain another three O levels.

In reality I only had a few weeks to prepare. I had lost a whole term whilst I was in hospital.

Just after the war an emergency training system was adopted. The country was desperately short of teachers many of whom had never returned from the war. At first the emergency training involved a twelve-month course during which teachers were trained, tested and sent out to teach.

Most of them were excellent. In fact I had one headteacher, one of the best teachers I met throughout the course of my career, who was emergency trained!

By 1952 things had settled down and a two-year teacher training programme was adopted. The year that O levels were introduced, it was decided that seven O levels would be enough to be accepted for teacher training.

I was eighteen years old on the 26th of August and I was therefore eligible to go to college in 1952. I did not need to spend another year at school, which is why I decided to take the short route. I planned to take another three O levels, English literature and art (which I would have taken as A levels) and religious knowledge.

I remember a lot of 'cramming' went on during the next few months. Besides trying to catch up with school work, I had lots of other things to catch up with. Firstly my duties including my prefecture and the vice captaincy of my house, Caedmon.

Obviously there was a life outside school as well. I was told on the grapevine that a boy called Cliff wanted to meet me. Cliff was a year ahead of me at school – in fact I believe he had left school to take up a draughtsman's apprenticeship. Then one day I was approached by a third former, pretty and blonde, who nervously handed me a letter. The girl was Anne and the letter was from her brother Cliff, telling me that he had admired me from afar for a long time. He ended by asking me to meet him.

To cut a long story short I eventually agreed to meet him and we met one Saturday evening on High Row, Darlington. This began a friendship that was to last until I went to college later that year.

Every Saturday evening without fail he would call at number 37 Greenbank Road to take me out, usually to the cinema. At other times he would call, sometimes bringing with him his golden retriever, and we would set off on one of the many walks in and around the town. I remember on one particular walk we had walked for miles out in the country and we were walking back down Nunnery Lane when Floss, my beautiful Border collie, decided to roll in a deposit left by a fox.

When we came to the road and I had to put her on a lead how I wish I'd had an extra-long lead. The smell was overpowering!

25

Sheila and I continued to spend as much time together as we could but we did not meet as regularly as we used to. Most weekends I was seeing Cliff and Sheila was also meeting a new boyfriend.

Sometime during that year Sheila and I managed to fit in a holiday to Hope in Derbyshire arranged by a company known as CHA Holidays. I'm not sure if it stood for Christian Holiday Association or Cooperative Holiday Association.

A step up from youth hostelling, we stayed in a beautiful house with many other, mainly young, people. Unlike youth hostels, meals were provided and activities were arranged. We enjoyed many of the activities and in doing so made many new friends. However, we also took days off on our own. We set off to explore the area around the village of Hope, which led us to discover caves!

Derbyshire is well known for its spectacular caverns, many of which are open to the public for a fee. It is also a place extremely popular with cavers and potholers. After visiting Speedwell Cavern and Peak Cavern we decided to do a bit of exploring ourselves. We were well used to difficult terrain when hiking and had even borrowed equipment and attempted to climb (under supervision) various rock faces. Potholing was something new! We obviously took advice from people who knew what they were doing and were invited to join one group to see if we liked it.

We were only on the holiday for two weeks and many days were taken up with arranged activities. Thus I think that probably we only spent four days exploring caverns. We thoroughly enjoyed the caving experience and fully intended at that time to pursue it further. However, I think we realised that the equipment alone would cost a bomb. Also my decision to go to college later that year put any future plans on hold.

26

I remember 1952 was a very busy year and the order in which things happened is a little bit hazy in my memory. I remember my time spent with Cliff. I remember working hard at school in preparation for exams. I remember my holiday in Derbyshire with Sheila. I remember a visit by Wally when we visited Richmond, Durham, York and Redcar and enjoyed a really wonderful time. I remember my eighteenth birthday. No big parties in those days, just a few friends came for tea.

I remember the excitement of packing a trunk with all the things I was going to need at college. I had a lovely bentwood cabin trunk which I think had been given to my mother by Lillian Thompson.

Looking back I have absolutely no recollection of how the cabin trunk made its way from my house to my room at Didsbury College. I presume the railway arranged delivery at the other end. Possibly Mr Saint, the taxi driver who lived next door, took it to the station for me. I really cannot remember!

All I do remember was that it appeared in my room at Didsbury College. Then came the weekend before I was due to travel to Manchester, to my new life, to my first time (apart from my hospital stay) living away from home. I was both excited and apprehensive at the same time. On the Saturday night I waited as usual for Cliff to arrive. He didn't! First time in over six months he didn't appear. Nor was there any explanation as to why.

(Actually to this day I have had no explanation as to what happened that night!) Mobile phones were not invented and very few people had telephones in their homes. The only person I knew who had a telephone was my friend Molly and of course Mr Saint the taxi driver who lived next door.

Previously, because it was my last night, friends had asked us to join them at the Palais. Cliff did not like dancing so we never took up the invitation.

However, as the hours passed with no appearance and no explanation, my mother suggested that I join my friends at the Palais. After all, it was my last night in Darlington for quite a while. I went to the Palais and met lots of people I knew, and I had a really enjoyable night.

I had danced with a boy called Geoff. He walked me home at the end of the evening and I remember when we got home we talked to my mother for quite a while. I learned later that Geoff had been quite concerned about how hard my mother worked and, after I went to college, used to regularly visit her and do jobs like bringing in the coal, sweeping the backyard etc. My mother thought the world of him.

That night was the end of a chapter. Tomorrow a whole new life was waiting for me.

27

My years at Darlington High School for Girls were happy ones. My teachers at primary school, especially Miss James (actually mainly Miss James), had steered me towards this time and prepared me well. However, it was a totally new learning experience.

No longer were we confined to sitting in one place for the whole day. Now at the end of one lesson we would move to a different place.

Laboratories, art rooms, gymnasiums, kitchens, sewing rooms, classrooms equipped for teaching specialist subjects such as French, geography etc.

Not only this but the school was set in beautiful surroundings. We had large playing fields and beautiful grassy areas in which we could just sit and relax.

Some members of staff really stand out in my memory whereas some others have faded totally from my mind. I think the teacher I remember most vividly in the early years is the chemistry teacher. I think her name was Miss Thompson. She was tall and stern with a strong Scottish accent.

I can still remember the very first lesson that I attended in the chemistry lab. We were seated in twos at benches containing a sink with a water tap. Next to that was a gas point from which a piece of rubber tubing led to a Bunsen burner. Each bench had a rack containing glass flasks, test tubes, Petri dishes etc.

I need to remember that we were all just eleven years old and totally overawed by our surroundings.

Miss Thompson introduced herself to us and in her usual stern manner lectured us on how we were to behave in her class. The first rule was 'to be observant'. The word "observant" was emphasised with loud strongly rolled 'rrr's'.

We were then instructed to watch her carefully and to be… 'obserrrrrrvant', and to do exactly what she did. She picked up a small white porcelain pot. She then held up her hand with her index finger pointing towards the ceiling and proceeded to show us her index finger. She then proceeded to dip her finger into the small pot she was holding in her other hand. She then placed her finger in her mouth and tasted whatever was in the pot with apparent relish!

The pot was then handed to the girl nearest to her and we were instructed to pass it around the class and to do exactly what she had done.

As the pot was passed around the class each girl dipped her finger into the pot and then into her mouth. The reaction of each girl was the same… total disgust at the taste.

When it reached the last girl, Miss Thompson took the small pot from her and returned to her bench.

With a smile on her face she said, "That might teach you to do as I say. You need to be obserrrrrrvant."

"Watch again!" She then proceeded to re-enact what she had actually done. First of all she showed us her index finger and waved it round the room so that we all saw it. She then dipped it into the liquid in the pot. She then once more pointed the finger to the ceiling and showed it to all the class. So far exactly what we had seen!

Then very slowly, so that we could see what she was doing, she changed that finger for her middle finger, and the middle finger was the one she put into her mouth.

I think we all learned two lessons that day – one was "to be observant" and the other one was that this teacher was one not to be messed with! I need to explain that the liquid in the pot was quinine!

I wasn't very good at chemistry. Possibly because I spent more time standing in the corridor having been sent out for giggling then I actually did in lessons. I remember the first time I was told to go and stand in the corridor. It was at the end of our first experiment and I have no idea what the substance was, but whatever it was, it was being heated in a test tube. We were working in pairs and I was the one who was gripping tongs holding the test tube over a Bunsen burner. Unfortunately my powder was the first to react and it shot out of the test tube like a rocket.

It came as such a shock that I screamed and dropped the tongs resulting in the glass test tube shattering all over the bench.

Hence I was sent to stand in the corridor. I remember spending many more chemistry lessons standing in the corridor, usually for laughing too much. It doesn't come as any surprise that my chemistry marks were always on the low side.

There was Miss MacPherson. Our very first form teacher. Always approachable, always kind and understanding.

I remember Miss Varley the Latin teacher. Again extremely strict and an excellent teacher. I really enjoyed her lessons. It was said that she had no sense of humour and people certainly did not mess around in her lessons! However, one day I discovered that she did have a sense of humour.

It was after school one day and Ann, myself and a couple of others were clearing up a mess that had been left in the classroom. I was taking a mop back to one of the cleaner's cupboards when I heard footsteps coming along the corridor.

I was sure it was one of my friends so as the footsteps reached the corner I leapt out in front of them brandishing my mop and shouting, "Boo!" Imagine my horror when I realised it was not one of my friends but Miss Varley. I think I froze on the spot! After what seemed an eternity, the totally unexpected happened – Miss Varley started to laugh!

I can't remember what she said to me but she was friendly and after a slight reprimand she sent me on my way. After that when we were in lessons she always gave me a little smile when our eyes met.

I remember Miss Morrell and also Mrs Fenton who taught PE and games. PE was one of the few subjects in which I shone. Certainly not games. But I loved PE.

I also adored Miss Morrell. She was young, pretty, and always friendly. She always praised me for my work and encouraged me to try new and more adventurous things. Often she would ask me to demonstrate exactly how it should be done to other pupils. How to climb a rope, how to balance on the beam and how to perform various vaults. Mrs Fenton was older but also an extremely nice teacher.

Sadly after I had left the school many years later I heard that Miss Morrell had developed polio and was in an iron lung! A truly tragic story.

Obviously I remember the headteacher, Miss Jewsbury. Again tall, stern, and seemingly unapproachable, but she was one of the most understanding, kind people that you could meet. She was extremely professional but always ready to listen.

Had it not been for her taking the trouble to visit me in hospital to talk to me about my future, and then to help me with my application, it is possible I would never have ended up at Didsbury College and my life and the lives of loads of other people close to me would have been very different.

Lots of other names come to mind.

Miss Bruin, who taught history. She had very little time for any girl she did not consider to be upper class. Probably for this reason I had very little interest in history when I was at school. It is only as I grew older that I realised how interesting it is to learn about the past.

Miss Howell, quite elderly with lily-white hair, taught geography. She had her favourites, I can't remember being one of them. Mrs Gibson who taught needlework. Again I was certainly not one of her favourites. Miss Lax, I remember her joy when I obtained an O level in maths. Miss Husband taught us English. A great teacher who taught me well, especially in English grammar. That school was where I grew up in so many ways.

It was where I developed from the little girl with two long pigtails, who arrived at school on the first day, dressed in a gymslip and long woollen stockings, excited, but totally lacking confidence and extremely nervous to be starting a new school, into a much more confident young lady. Gone were the pigtails. Gone was the gymslip.

All the teachers I have just mentioned helped to prepare me for life. They helped me to grow up. They helped to teach me right from wrong. They imparted all their knowledge, some of it stayed with me and some went straight over my head, but when they had finished I was ready to face the outside world. I have so much to thank them for.

28

The big day came. The day I was to start a new life. The day I was going to college.

I woke up that morning with a mixture of feelings, partly excitement, a great deal of apprehension and a certain amount of sadness.

Excitement that this was the first day of a new life, apprehension in that I was leaving my home and my mother where I felt safe and heading into totally unknown territory, and sadness because I was leaving my mother on her own.

I really can't remember how we got to the station, possibly we walked, possibly Mr Saint drove us there in his taxi. I don't even remember the journey. I just remember arriving at Didsbury College and being directed to my room.

I was met in the somewhat imposing entrance hall and taken down a long corridor. At one end of the corridor was the entrance to the men's wing, and at the far end the entrance to the women's wing which is where I was taken.

Beyond the door was another long corridor with rooms either side and towards the end of it was a staircase leading to the first floor. We walked along the corridor and climbed a flight of stairs at the end. Here again corridors stretched in front of me – one straight ahead and one to my right. We walked straight ahead and halfway along, stopped by a door on the left-hand side.

This was to be my room for the next year.

I remember thinking thank goodness there was a number on the door otherwise I should never find it again. Strangely enough, for the life of me I cannot remember that number now!

The room was small with a single bed by the wall down one side. A small chest of drawers and a tall narrow wardrobe, which I think had been reclaimed from various army barracks after the war, stood on the other side. A small table and one chair occupied the space in front of the window.

Standing in the middle of the room, upended, was my cabin trunk!

I just stood there, wondering two things. The first thing was, *what do I do next?* And the second one was, *what have I done? Do I really want to be a teacher?*

As I stood there with these doubts going round and round in my head, and wishing that I was back home, a door on the opposite side of the corridor opened and a voice said, "Hello. Thank goodness there's somebody else here!" I turned and saw a tall girl with a broad smile and she looked familiar! She then said, "Hang on, I think I know you!" We couldn't believe it. Her name was Helen. She was from Darlington and she was from my school.

I think I have already explained that because my birthday fell in August I was able to go to college at the end of the Lower VI. That was why we did not immediately recognise one another. Helen was a year ahead of me at school! We had never spoken to one another at school, but obviously passed from time to time in the corridor. It was nice to have somebody close by who had connections to my home and we became friends.

Later that day we met another girl from Darlington. Her name was Thelma. Thelma was the daughter of a doctor. She had attended a private school in the town called Polam Hall.

Thus our paths had never crossed. Helen and I were both – what I suppose you would call – working class, whereas Thelma was from a different world. She literally had no idea how to fend for herself in any way, not even how to make a cup of tea!

She was a sweet girl and we always helped her out when we could, but we were never in the same social circle. She had a boyfriend when she started college and I believe they were married soon after she finished college.

For the rest of that first day Helen and I explored our surroundings. We discovered that further down the corridor were toilets and showers. Next to the shower room was a small utility room with a large butler sink where we could wash our clothes. There was a countertop with a kettle so we were able to make hot drinks.

Further exploring discovered the common room, the refectory, a library and various lecture rooms including the main lecture theatre. In the lecture theatre, the desks were arranged in sloping tiers, each one looking down upon the stage where the lecturer would deliver his lectures. To sit at the very back of the class on the top tier was a little bit like looking down on a stage from the circle in a theatre.

I think we were both a little apprehensive as to what lay ahead.

Over the next two days and weeks we met many more of our fellow students. I can't remember all their names but certain ones stand out in my memory for different reasons. I remember a girl called Drusilla, Drew for short. She was one of the most outgoing, extroverted, gregarious girls I have ever known. I admired her greatly.

Then there was Brenda. An absolute beauty and a really nice girl to boot. I remember she paired up with a boy called Ted. They were inseparable for the two years that we were at college. From the beginning we knew that Ted had told her he had a girl at home and that they would be married when he finished his training. I think it's possible that Brenda always hoped that she could change his mind. I know she was madly in love with him. However at the end of the two years, he went home and married his girlfriend. I never did hear what happened to Brenda.

Then of course there was Hazel. She came from Durham. We became very good friends.

I think she had started to train as a nurse, but had changed her mind and come into teaching. She knew everything about the human body. Most of us were only eighteen and times were very different back then. Biology lessons never went into great detail, and lessons on sex were unheard-of. The things she taught us about the male anatomy!

Whereas the female contingent were mainly only just eighteen years old, male students were quite a few years older. This was because almost all of them had to do national service before they came to college. On the whole they were a really nice bunch of young men. Quite a few were day students, meaning that they lived at home and travelled into college each day.

A group of us soon became good friends and we spent many happy hours in one another's company, playing cards in the common room or just sitting in groups and chatting.

Of course it was absolutely forbidden females should enter the male wing or that males should set foot across the threshold of the female wing other than of course mothers or fathers or close relations. However, brothers and male cousins were eventually banned from admittance to the female wing. It was discovered that many girls thought that it was okay to take somebody else's brother into their room!

Of course it is quite natural for people anywhere to eventually settle into groups and we were no different. Our group of girls consisted of myself, Helen, Hazel, Drew, Brenda (when she wasn't with Ted), a girl called Marjorie and her friend Jean, and a girl called Margaret.

In the boys' (or should I say men's) group there was of course Ted and three boys from Blackpool, namely Alan (nickname Jack), Stan and Dave.

Not necessarily part of our group but always around were George, Harry (Harry was a little bit older than the rest of us) and a very, very tall young man called Ted.

At that time, unless we attended the same lectures, we had very little contact with the day students.

The first thing we had to do was decide on our chosen special subjects. We needed two subjects to study to advanced level. The rest of the subjects were compulsory. English language, psychology, and education (primary or secondary depending on our choice). From my specialist subjects I chose English literature and art and craft. I was really happy with my choices.

Thomas Hardy was amongst the list of authors that we could specialise in and he was my choice. In poetry I chose William Wordsworth. I remember both my English lecturers – one was named Seymour. I really liked him. He was kind and good at his job. I remembered him from my interview. He was my English language tutor. The work I produced for him nearly always resulted in a mark of either an A or A-. I loved his lectures.

My tutor for English literature was called Seabridge. Very different to Mr Seymour. A bit more pompous and certainly not as approachable. I think there were about ten of us in his group and after a couple of months we all began to notice that the mark we received for our very first assignment seemed to be the mark we were stuck with for the rest of time.

No matter how hard I tried, I came out with a C+ grade every time, and other members of the group noticed the same. It just seemed as though he decided on the very first encounter that that was what we were worth.

One member of our group was called Charlie. He was a day student, very well spoken, very smart, friendly, approachable and extremely clever. His very first assignment was given an A grade. Obviously it was worth it and after that it was an A grade every time.

I vividly remember on one occasion being in an absolute panic. I had spent the weekend enjoying myself instead of working and had forgotten all about a short essay which was to be handed in on the Monday afternoon. I must have discovered this when we were in the refectory and a group of us had got together and were chatting. Charlie was one of them. I can't remember what the assignment was, but I know that it was a very short assignment necessitating about a page of writing instead of the normal eight or ten pages. Charlie offered to sit down with me and we would do it together. This we did and thus I handed my work in on time. I was so grateful to him.

However, guess what, when the work was marked and handed back, even though I had been tutored and influenced by Charlie, the mark at the end was a C+.

My other main subject was art and craft and at the beginning I loved it. I'm racking my brains to try to remember the name of the tutor. I seem to remember the name Millichamp. I could be making that up or that could be the name of the tutor who was in charge of infant education.

However, whichever one it was kept changing her mind! She would give us a project to work on, then after a few days she would change it to something else. This often proved to be a bit of a nuisance but most of us accepted the fact she was a little eccentric and therefore we didn't complain too much.

However, something happened in the spring term which caused me to make a big decision, but I will talk about that later.

29

The first term at Didsbury was hard work but also a wonderfully exciting time in my life. The work was demanding but oh how I enjoyed the company.

Each evening after supper we girls would congregate in somebody's room where we would talk, laugh, gossip, sort out problems until it was late, sometimes very late, then in the early hours we would retire to bed.

There was also a café opposite the entrance gates where we would meet, as well as a cinema just down the road, and a fish and chip shop which had a small restaurant.

Obviously there were occasions when, as girls did, we discussed the students in the men's wing. I seem to remember that the Blackpool boys came top in popularity and were also considered to be the best looking with Alan rated to be the most handsome. He was the very epitome of 'tall, dark and handsome'!

I also remember there was a telephone! A luxury I had never ever been able to enjoy. Sometimes we would receive phone calls from home. Whoever was passing the cubicle when the phone rang would answer it and then proceed to track down the person that it was for.

If it was for someone in your own wing it was easy, but if it was somebody in the other wing it was a matter of standing at the door of the wing and shouting the name as loudly as possible until somebody heard.

Occasionally my mother would call, but it was easier for her to write a letter. A phone call meant a long walk to a public phone box. I had calls in the first few weeks from Cliff and also from Geoff. The conversations we had remain between me and them. The only thing I will say is that Cliff and I were no longer a couple.

It didn't take long before people started dating and I remember sitting there in absolute surprise and shock when Alan asked me if he could take me to the cinema. I was the first girl that he had asked to accompany him on a date and I was flattered beyond words.

Alan and I spent a lot of time together after that initial date. Trips to the cinema, fish and chip suppers, long walks and even trips into Manchester.

Of course almost all the males had done national service. They were young men not boys. We had fun but they treated us with respect at all times.

Times have changed a lot during my lifetime. But back then, when I was eighteen years old, we females were still treated like children and subjected to rules and regulations which would never be applied today.

All females had to be in by 10pm. If we wanted to stay out late at the weekends, for example when we went to one of the Manchester University union dances, then we had to apply for a late pass which allowed us to stay out until 10.30pm or even 11pm. For very special occasions this was sometimes extended to midnight, though very, very rarely.

On these occasions we were met at the door by whichever lecturer happened to be on duty that night. It was usually either Miss Mackay, the deputy principal, or Miss Hamer the PE lecturer. Both equally formidable. Even a few minutes late meant that we endured a severe reprimand.

What seemed to us girls to be so unfair, was that the same rules did not apply to the men.

As I previously stated most of them had just completed national service, which in some cases had included action in places like Malaysia.

Therefore I think it would have been totally impossible, and totally wrong, to treat them as children.

However, a few of the male students had come straight from school. They were allowed total freedom. No time limit was set for them. They could stay out until whatever hour they chose – no sex equality back then!

As time went on, we girls worked out different ways of sneaking into the building unnoticed. This was necessary when, for example, we had been to the cinema and the film finished late.

The windows in most of the girls' rooms were on the first floor, and those that were on the ground floor were at the front so it was impossible to sneak in that way without being seen. However! A very enterprising young man called Ted had worked out more than one way of making extra money while he studied.

His room was on the ground floor at the rear of the building, easy to access from the grounds, and difficult to be seen because there were no lights in that area.

Ted used to let us in through his window for a small charge of sixpence. Once inside it was still necessary to hide behind the door of the men's wing until the coast was clear. Only then were we able to exit and race along the corridor to the safety of our own wing.

Talking about Ted and some of the little schemes he had going reminds me of something else about that first term.

After completing two or three years of national service most of the male students were smokers. It didn't take long for those of us who had just left school to be tempted to try what was then considered to be quite sophisticated. Everywhere you looked advertisements made smoking seem the most glamorous, sophisticated activity to be part of.

Hence after a lot of coughing and choking quite a few of us were addicted. We didn't smoke very many, obviously we couldn't afford to, but this is where Ted came in. He used to buy packets of cigarettes and sell them one at a time for 2d.

If his male counterparts needed a cigarette they would simply knock on his door, whereas we females had to knock on the door of the male wing, open it slightly and shout Ted's name loudly.

So besides offering a route into the building late at night, Ted kept us supplied with all sorts of things, including cigarettes which he sold at a profit. I would imagine that he eventually became a millionaire.

As for the smoking, none of us could afford to buy whole packets of cigarettes. However, as a real treat I would buy a packet of Du Maurier. The design of the packets was different to the normal cigarette packets. They had a flip-up lid and went with the sophisticated appearance that we were all searching for.

However, smoking was something that I had to keep from my mother for many years. She would have been furious!

After a few weeks Alan and I 'moved on'. He was extremely serious, not a lot of humour, whereas I found humour in most things and would dissolve into uncontrollable fits of laughter at the slightest thing.

I think I slowly came to the realisation that humour was an important part of my life. It was all very well feeling quite special to be going out with the most handsome boy in college, but at what cost? It was probably then that I realised that was exactly what I had been doing back home in Darlington. Cliff didn't have a great sense of humour but he was extremely tall and handsome.

Laughter was important in my life. At school it was something that had got me into trouble year after year and yet I was unable to control it. If something was funny I had to laugh… even if it was inappropriate!

I went out a couple of times with Stan, another one of the Blackpool boys, and with Don who was in the year ahead of us. As we settled into college life, we became braver and more adventurous. Saturday night we ventured into Manchester to Manchester University union dances.

These were enjoyable and we met other people. I met up a couple of times with a student name Tom. A medical student at the university studying to be a doctor. He took me home a couple of times and even came to the college to pick me up and take me to the cinema on one occasion.

I vividly remember one occasion when a young man I'd been dancing with at the beginning of the evening asked me if he could give me a lift home. I was thrilled because this meant I could stay at the dance for longer. I didn't need to leave to catch the bus. I willingly accepted and at the end of the evening we left the dance together and walked down the road and I expected to see a car. I couldn't believe my eyes when we stopped beside a motorbike!

Imagine the picture, a full billowing skirt, a lacy shawl around my shoulders, no hat or helmet! However, I had no option… face the trouble I would be in if I was late (and it wouldn't be five minutes late, more like two hours), or risk a ride on the back of the bike. I risked the ride and made it on time even though I arrived back at college looking as though I had been through a blizzard!

At the end of that we all went home for Christmas. This time I had companions to travel with on the train, namely Helen and Thelma.

It felt great to be home. Great to see my mother. Even my grandmother was pleased to see me. It was so, so good to snuggle down in my comfortable bed (the beds at college were not particularly comfortable).

Obviously I was also looking forward to catching up with my friends back home and bringing them up to date. They all wanted to know what college life was like and I was obviously enjoying it so much that both Liz and Sheila – both of whom up till then had no idea what they wanted to do in the future – decided then and there that they wanted to go to teacher training college.

I won't go into great details because some things are too personal to talk about to other people, but Cliff and I met on a couple of occasions during that Christmas break after which we ceased all contact. Let me just say I do not react well to constant sarcasm. However, we parted as friends and sixty-six years later through the medium of Facebook and Cliff's grandson, we were in contact again and continue to be so until this day.

30

I had a great Christmas, and New Year was celebrated in the usual way. The year 1953 had arrived and I returned to college. I soon settled back into the college routine and worked hard to keep up with my college work.

Various groups and clubs were successfully organised and ran throughout the college year. Drama, singing, rambling, book clubs, gymnastics and many more. I thoroughly enjoyed the gymnastics club and the drama group.

One of my favourite pursuits had always been walking in the great outdoors and one day I spotted a notice on the noticeboard with information about a forthcoming ramble to Kinder Scout. I put my name down and looked forward to the walk very much.

Sheila and I had explored the areas around Hope and Castleton but never had time to explore Kinder Scout.

The day arrived for the trip and I gathered with a group of students near the gate to wait for our transport. The details of how we financed the trip, whether it was public transport, or whether we hired the coach, are quite blurred in my mind. I do remember boarding a small coach and choosing a seat near the front beside the window.

The next moment a young man with a mop of blond hair and a cheeky grin pushed past the people standing in the aisle trying to decide where to sit, and flopped into the seat beside me. Due to the fact that he was one of the day students, our paths had not crossed before. He introduced himself and we began to chat. We chatted all the way to our destination. His name was Derek. Derek Clegg.

Little did I guess, as we sat and chatted, that this was the first day of the rest of my life.

We eventually arrived at our destination and we all got off the coach. I remember it was a sunny day and very, very cold! There was a covering of snow on the higher ground which made the glorious scenery look even more beautiful.

In the same way that Sheila and I, and others, had explored the Dales and the moors of North Yorkshire, Derek knew the Peak District like the back of his hand.

As we walked Derek told me that he knew a much shorter route than the one the group were following. He suggested that he and I took the 'shortcut' and met up with the group again at a certain point. I agreed to go along with him.

I think a circular route from the car park at Edale was about ten miles. We were all well equipped. After all it was wintertime and there was snow on the ground.

Derek and I both had proper hiking boots and thick socks. Clothing was warm and waterproof. We carried spare clothing, e.g. socks and extra jumpers, in our small rucksacks. Derek even had a small ice axe hanging from the back of his rucksack.

The circular walk normally took between four and five hours. The route Derek had chosen was very enjoyable, though it was not easy, indeed it was quite challenging at times. It was often necessary to traverse small streams and usually these were crossed safely and without incident. However, shortly before the point where we had agreed to meet the rest of the party, it was necessary to cross yet another stream. This stream was wider than the others and in full flow. Several large rocks protruded from the water and it was necessary to use those as stepping stones. Derek went across first. He then shouted to me to throw my rucksack across to him. I successfully threw it and he caught it – so far so good!

I then proceeded to make the crossing myself and was successful until I reached the last stone before the bank on the other side. The distance between the stone and the bank was considerable. Too far for me to stride! Derek's advice was for me to jump! I jumped… but I didn't make it! I landed knee-deep in icy-cold water. I remember feeling so stupid as Derek hauled me out on the other side. I was absolutely freezing.

We were very close to the point where we had arranged to meet up with the rest of the group who had taken a slightly longer route to get there, so we found a sheltered spot behind some large boulders with a convenient flat stone for us to sit on. I was able to put on warm, dry socks. However, I don't think I have ever felt so cold. Derek did his best to keep me warm by hugging me tightly whilst we waited for the rest of the party to arrive. When they arrived I admit I felt a bit stupid, but my news was met with a mixture of amusement and sympathy and we continued the walk all together. We arrived back to the car park cold and tired and, apart from the leap into cold water, having had a really enjoyable and eventful day.

As I have already stated, although at the time I did not know it, this was the first day of the rest of my life.

31

A few days later I attended a lecture in the lecture theatre at college. As I entered the room Derek, who was sitting towards the back of the theatre, saw me and came rushing down the steps to greet me.

I remember everybody laughing when he bowed low with a flourish and said, "Will you be my life's companion?" I sat beside him for the lecture and met two of his friends, also day students, namely Geoff and Patrick.

After that we always sat together for any lectures which involved all students. Derek and I spent a lot of time together in the following weeks. Quite often, instead of going home after his last lecture, he would stay on and we would sit in the common room chatting. We went for walks, visited the cinema, and sometimes even ventured into Manchester to attend a students' union dance.

I so enjoyed his company. He was a breath of fresh air. He could turn anything into humour and we laughed a lot.

Also I was in awe of his intelligence, and his knowledge. I had never met anybody, apart from Wally my Belgian friend, with such a brain.

I discovered that Derek had just spent four years (I think

it was four years) in the RAF. Called up to do his national service, he had opted to join the RAF. There are quite a few stories that he told me about his time in the RAF.

On the first day he met a young man called Tony Britton. They got on well together and when it came to allocating accommodation Tony Britton suggested that they had more in common than any of the others and suggested that they shared. I understand they became pretty good friends during that time in the RAF, yet they failed to stay in touch when it was all over. Tony went on to become quite famous in various television roles as an actor.

Derek enjoyed his time doing national service and at the end of it was persuaded to stay on, in other words to sign on for another couple of years during which time he would be taught how to fly.

How I wish he was here to be able to relay some of the things he experienced during that time.

One thing I do remember him telling me was about his experiences in a Tiger Moth. I think it was his first solo flight.

He had done really well and was feeling very confident as he came in to land. However, just before the wheels touched the runway, a tremendous gust of wind tipped the plane over and he actually landed upside down.

Not very good for your street cred and certainly not something to make your instructor happy!

Derek ended up obviously shaken, severely bruised with a broken forearm and a broken nose.

A great deal of fuss was obviously made about the Tiger Moth which had been somewhat damaged in the unconventional landing, but this was the services! People were expected to be tough, not to complain and just get on with it!

Therefore neither the arm nor the nose received any attention and were left to 'heal themselves'. Derek lived the rest of his life with a slightly wonky forearm and a slightly bent nose. Most people who met him thought he had been a rugby player in the past.

During this time Derek was also expected to do some lecturing to new recruits. He found this was something he really enjoyed doing, something he looked forward to and something he found extremely rewarding.

Before he went into the RAF Derek had been working for a firm called Simon Carves – a big engineering company. He was well thought of and a promising career in engineering was on the cards. He spent some time on work experience at a steelworks in Middlesbrough.

However, his love of lecturing whilst he was in the RAF caused him to do an about-turn with his career. He applied to Didsbury College to train to become a teacher, and turned his back on engineering.

Therefore both he and I started our first term at Didsbury College in September 1952, though we didn't meet until the spring of 1953.

We had been dating for about three weeks when we decided to go into Manchester to one of the student union dances. I can still remember that evening. That was the evening that Derek told me he loved me and asked me to marry him. I remember being in total shock. Marriage was something that had never crossed my mind. I'd never even thought that one day I might meet somebody, fall in love, get married and possibly raise a family. I didn't know what to say.

I was flattered. I was extremely happy to know that he loved me, but I couldn't give him a reply. It's so long ago now that I can't remember exactly what we said, but I know that Derek was happy to give me time.

We continued to spend as much time together as possible. I loved the time we spent together and I missed him when he wasn't there. I was falling in love, and I think it scared me a little!

I remember the first time Derek took me home to introduce me to his mother and his stepfather. Derek's father had been diagnosed with cancer shortly after Derek joined the RAF. Derek's mum was nursing him at home. One day Derek was summoned and given the sad news that his father was dying.

He was given compassionate leave and provided with travel documents to get him home as quickly as possible. Sadly his father passed away while Derek was on his way home. That must have been very hard to bear. Shortly after that Derek's mum married Fred.

On that first meeting Fred was extremely friendly and welcoming, but Derek's mum Gertie was quite aloof, bordering on hostile. At the time I put it down to nerves.

He also took me to meet his Aunt Doris and his Uncle Ernie. (Doris was Derek's father's sister.) They were so friendly and welcoming and went out of their way to make me feel at home. They were both to become extremely important people in my life. I came to love them dearly.

Life was busy at college during that spring term, but I will move on to the Easter break and come back to that later.

When the Easter break came I, along with Helen and Thelma, boarded the train to go home to Darlington. It was the first time Derek and I had been apart for an extended period for many weeks. We wrote to one another daily and I can remember to this day how happy I was the day I answered a knock on the front door, to find Derek standing there with his bicycle. He had cycled all the way from Stockport in Cheshire to my home in Darlington. One side of the country to the other and over the Pennines.

I think it was about 130 miles each way. Perhaps I should say at this point that Derek was a keen cyclist. He had a beautiful racing bike and often used to cycle in the Peak District.

It was nothing to him to leave home for an evening ride and do a round trip past the Cat and Fiddle Inn, the second highest pub in the country at that time, and home again. A round trip of almost forty miles.

I was delighted to see him and he was welcomed not just by me but by my mother, and by my grandmother who couldn't get over the fact that he had come all that way on a bicycle. I still remember her words to me as she whispered in my ear, "That must be love!"

My mother and myself quickly sorted out bedding and made up a bed for him in the bedroom which was only ever used when visitors stayed over.

The next few days were spent with me showing Derek my hometown.

One day we had been for a long walk and we were walking by the river. I suddenly knew that I couldn't bear to ever let him go. The love I felt at that moment was different to anything I'd ever felt before. In that moment I knew that my answer was going to be, "Yes."

So I just said it. "Yes! I will marry you. I love you." I can't remember what we said next. I just remember in the excitement of the moment we narrowly avoided falling into the river!

That night we told my mum and my grandmother. We assured my mother that nothing had changed. We still intended to finish our college course and gain our teaching certificates. After that we would wait until it was financially viable before we married.

After a few days I remember waving him off as he started his long cycle ride back to Stockport.

I would be travelling back to Manchester a few days later and then, and only then, would I know if he had arrived home safely. We didn't have telephones back then and a letter wouldn't arrive before I had left for college.

However, any worries I had about him reaching home safely disappeared as my train pulled into Manchester station. There he was, waiting on the platform to meet me!

32

Back to other things which happened during that spring term. I continued to do well in most of my college work. My A grades in English language kept coming, though C, C+ and occasionally a B- continued with my work in English literature.

My work in art and craft continued to achieve good grades. It was something I enjoyed immensely and I certainly received a lot of praise and encouragement from the lecturer. I still can't remember her name.

However, one particular assignment necessitated the making of puppets. I have some vague recollection that our lecturer wanted us to put on a special display and I remember the puppets I was asked to make were of Prince Charming and his footman. I was given detailed instructions as to the costumes for example, style, colour, adornment etc.

I spent hours and hours making them. I was meticulous about the detail. I searched for rich velvet, and crisp lace in the requested colours. I took care with every detail – buttonholes, buttons and belts, even the eyelashes and the hair – and I was so pleased with the outcome. However, to achieve this I had had to work late into the night for weeks in order for them to be ready to hand in by the deadline. The date came, and we all duly presented our work. She was absolutely delighted with my puppets. They were held up as an example of beautiful work and I was so thrilled to have pleased her so much.

That weekend Derek and I were able to actually enjoy a day out in the country as I had caught up with all my work.

Monday morning came and I had a message requesting me to go to see the art and craft lecturer. I went to see her and I couldn't believe the sight that awaited me. On the large table were my puppets… in pieces… every stitch had been unpicked!

She was actually smiling. I don't think I was really hearing what she said, I was just in such shock.

She explained that she had changed her mind and that the display was going to represent a totally different period and that my puppets were so good that it wouldn't take me long to make others in a different style.

As she spoke I remember she gathered together all the pieces and gave them to me, smiling all the time.

The next thing I remember was standing outside the door holding all the bits of my puppets with instructions to make new ones.

It was then that the anger set in. Even if she had changed her mind, why was it necessary to destroy the puppets that I had already made? The puppets I had spent so much time on. The puppets that she had gone into raptures about two days before. Why not just ask me to make some more?

Changing her mind halfway through a project was nothing new. She was noted for it. But this, this was a step too far. I didn't even stop to think things through. I just decided there and then that I no longer wished to be part of that class.

Propelled by anger I found myself knocking on the principal's door and obeying the command, "Come in." Once inside the room Mr Body asked me to take a seat, which I did. I really at that moment in time had no idea what I was going to say, but I must have said quite a lot, because when I left that room, art and craft was no longer one of my chosen subjects.

As it turned out there was only one other option available to me, and I had taken it. From that moment on my second chosen specialist subject was – and I still find it difficult to say this – mathematics!

Mathematics never has been and never will be a subject that I find easy. My maths teacher, Miss Lax, would have laughed till the tears rolled down her face if she knew what I had just done. I can still remember her delight mixed with absolute disbelief when I added mathematics to my list of O levels.

I find as I get older that people's names are the first thing to disappear from my memory. In some cases I suddenly remember them, but in others, even if I can still remember their face, the name has been totally obliterated from my memory. Somewhere in the back of my mind lurks the name of the maths lecturer.

The man who was so good at his job that he actually steered me through the two-year course of mathematics that I needed to pass in order to get my teaching certificate.

His patience and his generosity with his time got me through. But it wasn't just that, he was the first person that had taken the trouble to sit down with me and explain things. And time after time something that had seemed to me to be utter gobbledygook, suddenly fell into place and I understood it perfectly. Once I understood 'why' then I was able to solve problems related to that particular aspect of mathematics.

The closest I can get to his name was Mr Cresswell and that is how I will refer to him from now on. I am angry with myself that I am uncertain about his name because I owe him so much.

I think it was during that spring term that we performed our first school practice which involved facing a class of children and trying to put into practice all we had been taught so far.

My first school was called Halton Bank in Salford.

I can't remember how I ever found my way there. It was left to us to sort out which number bus we needed, consult a timetable and find our way to the school under our own steam.

That first day of school practice was a day I shall never forget. What on earth had I let myself in for? What was I doing here?

Up till now I had had absolutely no contact with small children and here I was surrounded by about forty-six of them all seemingly demanding attention at the same time.

Somehow, goodness knows how, I managed to get through two weeks of torture. Two weeks of desperately trying to create order out of chaos. Two weeks of trying to ensure that I attended to the needs of every single child in my care.

I don't remember too many details about that time, but I do remember one occasion when one of our tutors came to watch me and report back on my progress.

A great part of the day in those days was allocated to 'activities'. A time where children were divided into groups, each group performing a totally different activity. Obviously when the teachers were in charge, day after day everything ran like clockwork. However, when we students took over things were very different! Organised chaos was a much better way of describing it.

At the end of the lesson the tutor took me to one side to tell me what she thought of my lesson, and to give me advice on the many ways I could improve. She pointed out that I had totally ignored a young child who was trying to show me his painting. She pointed out that my refusal to acknowledge and appreciate his work could have damaging effects on his development.

I had remembered the child! I remembered that I had commended him on his painting on the first couple of times that he had shown it to me. I also remembered that he showed it to me many, many more times. I also remember that eventually being followed around the room with a painting being waved in my face constantly, no matter how many times I said it was very good, became a bit of a nuisance. I remembered that I had taken the painting from the child (probably in a very impatient manner) and put it with other finished paintings in a pile on top of the bookshelf.

I sincerely hope that my actions that day did not cause a little boy to suffer from mental stress for the rest of his life!

During the summer term we took part in a pageant. Looking back now, with my hazy memory, I imagine it was something to do with the coronation. I think the whole thing was being organised by the university and all schools and colleges who were connected to the university in some way took part.

The theme was connected to history through the ages, hence we were dressed in varying forms of costume, each one representing a different age. I had been selected to represent the Tudor age and I was partnered by George. Derek on the other hand represented the Georgian age and he was partnered by Drusilla (I remember he looked extremely smart in his Georgian costume).

Also various outings were arranged by the college, including a visit to the Manchester Ship Canal.

I remember this because it rained solidly for the whole day and I have photographs, taken on the coaches, and the canal boats, showing us all looking like drowned rats!

We eventually came to the end of our first year. We were going to be allocated different rooms in our second year so everything had to be stored safely. Fortunately my cabin trunk held a considerable amount.

All my books including all the textbooks I had bought from various second-hand bookshops in Manchester, and all my notebooks and coursework were carefully packed away.

The last day of term arrived and we left for home. We said goodbye to the second year students who had finished their training, gained their certificates and were about to start new careers.

33

That summer holiday in 1953 was a wonderful time in my life. We had decided that we would return home, search for work and hopefully end up with decent holiday jobs, after which we would take a holiday somewhere.

My first job was in a hotel in Darlington. If my memory serves me right it was called the Imperial Hotel. It stood on the corner of a crossroads close to the town centre, opposite the Greentree Café.

My job there was a chambermaid. As a student I wasn't considered good enough to be let loose on the guests' bedrooms, so I was given the job of cleaning rooms tucked away in the top corner of the building which were used by resident staff.

Chefs, waiters and headwaiters were amongst the staff who occupied these rooms. At first everything went well, though on one occasion I was called back to one of the bathrooms because I hadn't cleaned the bath properly! But apart from that my work seemed to be satisfactory.

However, on one occasion I entered a room, certainly not expecting to see what I saw! The room was occupied by the head barman. He had worked long into the night and had been rewarded with 'time off'. As I entered the room, complete with mop and bucket and other accessories, I was greeted by a sight that is hard to forget. A man stood in the middle of the room, absolutely stark naked. On hearing me enter the room, he turned, smiled, stretched out his arms and said, "Come in, hinny. You and I can have some fun." Needless to say I fled! I don't think I dropped my bucket, but I was shocked enough to possibly have done so!

Strangely enough I decided to leave that job and find employment elsewhere.

My next job was in the Odeon Cinema, selling ice creams in the interval. It was not well paid. Wages consisted of a minimal amount per week topped up by commission on the amount of ice cream sold. I think that my basic wage was seven shillings and sixpence per week.

There were two seating areas in cinemas back then. Upstairs and downstairs. Seats upstairs were more expensive. As the newcomer I was given the upstairs position to sell my ice creams. Evidently because people had paid more money to sit upstairs they spent less on refreshments.

Back in the '50s there were intervals between the films and we always had two films. The main film and a second less well-known movie, known these days as a B-movie.

My instructions were that I had to be in place when the film ended and the lights came up in the cinema.

My 'place' was at the bottom of the staircase next to the balcony facing the audience. I still remember the shock I felt when I was presented with my tray for carrying the ice creams I was expected to sell.

Usherette trays, as they were known, were quite large with a strap which hung from the neck. The tray was filled with ice-cream tubs and in the centre was a tin full of loose change. I could hardly lift it and when it was hanging around my neck it appeared to weigh twice as much.

My instructions were that I had to reach my 'place' and be in position ready to sell my wares before a spotlight, positioned to shine directly on me, was switched on just before the main lights in the cinema came up. I was to achieve this quietly, without drawing any attention to myself!

I don't remember the title of the film that was showing but I do remember that it had a very tense, slightly scary ending.

Hence as I began my first tentative steps down the staircase, the audience were gripped by the tension of the film. They were either hanging on tightly to their partner, or to the arms of the seat in which they were sitting. You could hear a pin drop. Nobody moved. You could cut the tension with a knife.

I continued to make my way down the staircase and then it happened! I misjudged a step, caught my heel on the edge and staggered forward. As I did so most of the things in my tray, including the loose change in the tin, leapt upwards and crashed downwards, creating a tremendous noise!

The reaction of the audience was absolute shock. People literally jumped out of their seats, and many emitted a loud shriek. I think I froze to the spot for what seemed like an age but what probably was only a few seconds. Then as quietly as I could I tried to retrieve the few ice-cream tubs that had fallen to the floor, although most of them had continued rolling down the steps.

It's all a bit of a blur as to how I actually reached my 'spot' at the front of the balcony. However, somehow I made it. The spotlight came on and I tried, oh how I tried, to compose myself. However, the worst moment was yet to come. The moment when all the cinema lights came on and I was able to see all the faces that were staring at me! The worst thing was I actually knew some of them! I don't think that I have ever felt so stupid as I did at that moment. Somehow I did survive, and I actually kept my job, surprise, surprise!

At the end of each interval I returned my tray, remaining ice creams were counted, the money in my tin was counted (I hate to think how much I lost on the floor on my first day) and I went to sit in the staffroom until the next interval.

The staffroom was full of other people employed in the cinema, mainly usherettes and ice-cream sellers. I was just grateful that my job was only for a few weeks. As we only worked during intervals, most of the time between the films was spent sitting in this tiny staffroom.

To compensate for the boredom most of the regular staff played cards. They played cards for money and many of them repeatedly lost what little they had earned to the few who seemed to be experts at whichever game it was they were playing. I don't think I was popular because I turned down their invitation to take part.

I managed to keep this job despite my disastrous start. I didn't have much choice as there were no other jobs going at that time, apart from the one in the hotel!

Derek also found work. He managed to find work at Pickering's Pea factory. It was one of those jobs where you were taken on as casual labour. It necessitated turning up early each day at a specific place. A supervisor would come out and allocate people to various jobs around the factory. When all those jobs were filled, all the people not chosen that day had to go home until the next day when they would return to try again.

In the first few days of being there Derek was fortunate enough to be chosen for mundane jobs like packing! He discovered that jobs which needed experience or specific knowledge (and were often better paid because of this) were called out first. So whatever the job was he decided that he would put his hand up!

One day the supervisor asked if anybody had ever driven a tractor. Derek's hand shot up! The upshot was that on the first day he hit a barn door and demolished part of a dry stone wall in the farmyard. Needless to say he didn't keep that job for long.

A few days later the supervisors asked the question, "Anybody here know anything about physics?" Derek was delighted having never received anything less than an A grade in any physics exam. It was an easy choice for the supervisor as Derek was the only one with his hand up. He was taken to a room and his job was explained.

Sacks of peas which had been selected from a particular batch were brought into the room and Derek was asked to test them to see at which pressure they burst.

Anything which burst below a certain pressure was to be discarded, whereas anything which gained a certain pressure before it burst was okay and could be sent for processing.

I think that was right although with my limited knowledge of physics it could be the other way round.

Whichever way it was Derek set to work. (According to Derek no knowledge of physics was necessary in order to work the simple machine he was given.)

A couple of hours after Derek had begun work the door burst open and an extremely flustered supervisor from the processing department came into the room demanding to know what the ****** **** was going on?! It seemed that the whole of the processing department had been brought to a standstill because no peas were arriving for processing. Sack after sack after sack was being discarded.

I understand that Derek explained that he was just obeying instructions. I believe it was then explained to him in very colourful language that he did not need to be so ****** exact. Approximately nine out of ten sacks were being discarded, and at that rate the company would soon go out of business!

Needless to say Derek did as he was told and became much more lenient with the number of sacks that he allowed through. I must admit that we never ate processed peas from a can ever again!

He kept that job for the next few weeks and eventually the day that we had decided we would stop working arrived. Derek would come up to Darlington and we would plan a holiday. I remember him arriving, one of the few times he arrived by train, and I was so pleased to see him.

Derek had been quite well paid whilst he was working, whereas I had very little to show for what had been hard work. Unknown to me Derek had already organised a holiday.

When we had agreed to marry we had also agreed to make our engagement official at the end of our first year at college. Derek had arranged to take me to one of his favourite places which was the town of Oban in Scotland.

I must admit I was really excited at the prospect of going on holiday, especially to stay in a hotel, as in the past it had always been boarding houses. However, I found returning to Scotland a little daunting after what had happened a couple of years previously. I said nothing of this to Derek, and if I'm honest the excitement was certainly greater than any apprehension.

But before that there was the question of the ring. We visited a jewellers on High Row Darlington on the corner of Post House Wynd. Even though Derek had worked hard and earned considerably more than I did, funds were still quite tight and I think the ring was one of the cheapest we could find. But its value was not important, I loved it.

A few days later we boarded a train heading for Scotland. The journey itself was wonderful. I knew the journey to Edinburgh, which followed the north-east coast, very well, having travelled it many times before when we visited Edinburgh. The rest of the journey the scenery was great, especially the closer we got to Oban.

Derek had booked us into a hotel where he had stayed as a child. When he was a little boy, Derek's Auntie Flo, who was married to a man called Fred Messenger, used to often take Derek with her on their travels.

Florence, Auntie Flo, was Derek's dad's eldest sister. She and Fred did not have any children and compared to the rest of the family were quite well off.

Here I go again having problems with names. I think the hotel was the Royal Hotel. I can remember exactly what it looked like but the name is a bit hazy, so let's call it the Royal.

I remember arriving at the hotel and approaching the desk at reception. I remember also the lady who greeted us at the reception desk. I cannot say that the greeting was a very friendly one, in fact it was anything but. Derek gave her our names and told her that we had just become engaged and had two rooms reserved for the next week. Her manner and the way she spoke to us made it perfectly obvious that she very much disapproved of a young man and a young woman going on holiday together before they were married.

She called another employee of the hotel and instructed him to show Derek to his room. She then proceeded to show me my room. The Royal was a large hotel, bigger than anything I had ever stayed in before. My room was at one end of the hotel, Derek's at the other end of the hotel and we were on different floors. If either one of us had attempted to visit the other in their room it meant passing the reception desk and there was always somebody on duty. Once we said goodnight there was absolutely no contact until the following day. Remember mobile phones had not been invented. I remember feeling quite anxious as I didn't even know where Derek's room was.

Also the hostile reaction from the receptionist brought back vivid memories of that night on Loch Lomond when Sheila and I experienced such hostility.

For that reason I think I went to sleep that night with the light still on. I was awoken at about 6am by somebody hammering on my door shouting, "Your light is still burning," in a very strong Scottish accent. "It costs money!"

The next morning I eventually found my way to the dining room where I found Derek waiting for me. Despite the attitude of the receptionist and whoever had hammered on my door at 6:30am accusing me of wasting money (I actually think they were one and the same) the staff in the dining room were delightful and we enjoyed breakfast and dinner each and every day. We spent each day visiting a different place, sometimes aboard a MacBrayne ferry, one of the many ferries which sailed between the islands and up and down the coast. Each evening after dinner we took a walk and explored Oban itself. Like Derek had all those years before when he was a boy, I too fell in love with Oban and the area.

When we eventually boarded the train to take us home I felt a mixture of sadness and delight in the knowledge that one day I would return.

A wonderful way to celebrate our engagement, all down to the fact that Derek had worked so hard. I'm not sure that what I earned was even enough to pay for the many cups of tea, plates of scotch pancakes, drop scones and ice creams that we enjoyed on a daily basis.

34

At the end of an incredible week we finished the holiday as we had begun, by enjoying the wonderful scenic train journey back to Darlington. After a few more days it was time for Derek and I to say goodbye for a while. I waved him off from the platform at Darlington station. Over the next couple of weeks we wrote letters every other day – strangely enough, back in the '50s, we may not have had telephones, let alone mobile phones, but letters did arrive on time!

Before we broke up for the summer holidays at the end of our first year, Derek had applied to become a resident for his second and final year. His application was successful and he moved into residence. I'm trying to remember if his friend Geoff moved into residence as well, but no matter how hard I try I can't remember. I do know that his special friend Patrick did not. Pat was married and lived with his wife Nancy in Hyde, a small Cheshire town. On numerous occasions we were invited by Pat and Nancy to spend the weekend with them in their home.

During our second year we were all allocated new rooms. I was still located on the first floor but this time when I reached the top of the stairs I turned right and my room was the first on the right. This time I was surrounded by all the special friends I had made – Hazel and Margaret to name but two.

This second and final year was a very important year. A lot of hard work was packed into a short space of time. Besides working towards final exams at the end of the year we also had three more school practices to complete.

Days were spent attending lectures, catching up with coursework, completing assignments, congregating in the kitchen or somebody's room to catch up with the latest gossip, and even writing letters home.

Evenings were spent meeting up in the common room, or attending one of the many clubs that were available. Derek and I were still members of the rambling club. The rambling club organised many trips, often into Derbyshire, and we always took part in anything connected to walking or camping.

I also kept up my love of gymnastics by joining the gym club.

There was also a rock climbing club organised by a young man called Mike. There were many weekend climbs involving various degrees of difficulty in the Derbyshire Peak District. Derek was quite good at climbing and one day he persuaded me to join him on a day out into Derbyshire where a climb had been arranged. I was pretty agile and I could skim up a rope at high speed, so off I went thinking that this would be a doddle. I did okay for a while and for the first few visits I managed to negotiate climbs quite well. Then one day Mike decided that we would attempt a much more ambitious climb. We set off. I was one of the last to begin the climb and at first I was doing quite well, but then towards the top of the climb I came to a point which necessitated a jump to catch hold of what was known as a jug in order to position myself to complete the climb. I was fully roped up but even so, looking down, it was an awful long way to the ground, and the thought of letting go with both hands, hurling myself into space and trusting myself to safely grab hold of 'the jug' was terrifying! I froze. I just couldn't move. What happened next is a bit hazy in my mind but I do know that it necessitated Mike coming back down to me and holding me while the rest of the group hauled us both to the top. To say that I was embarrassed is putting it mildly. Everybody was very nice and said it could happen to anybody. I suppose it could but I didn't want that anybody to be me.

I did accompany the group after that now and again but if a climb involved leaping for a jug or traversing an overhang, I never took part. I met them all at the top! But enough about leisure time for the moment. Let me get back to the serious stuff.

Early in that autumn term came the next school practice. This time I was sent to a school in Gorton. It was the most depressing place. Each classroom had huge windows but far too high for anybody, including the teacher, unless you were over six feet tall, to actually see anything more than the sky!

My class consisted of about forty-five children aged between six and seven years.

I remember turning up the first day, all lessons and activities fully prepared, praying that this experience would be better than the last one in Salford. The teacher introduced me to the class and stayed with me throughout the first day, helping me to find my way round the school, showing me where stock was kept, and acquainting me with any special problems a particular child might have.

I went back to college that day feeling much more confident that this time it was going to be so much better than it was in Salford. I think I was very naive back then.

The next day the teacher taught for the first hour. I took over after the morning playtime. Fully prepared, everything I needed at my fingertips, what could go wrong?! Everything!

As soon as the teacher left the room and the door closed, sweet little children morphed into something resembling wild animals. Once again I wondered why on earth I had ever thought that I wanted to teach!

I'm not sure whether during those two weeks anyone's child actually learnt anything!

I was just extremely grateful that I managed to keep them alive and free from injury, and also that the headcount was the same when I handed them back to the teacher as it was when I took control.

One of my most vivid memories was a PE lesson I took on that particular school practice. The lesson was to be taken outside in the playground. We were expected to include the use of all available equipment in the lesson. The most humiliating part was that not only were the children expected to strip to vest and pants, we the teachers had to change into T-shirt and shorts too!

I need to set the scene…

Many parts of Manchester still showed signs of the aftermath of war; many bomb sites had been cleared but not reused, therefore there were vast open spaces of nothing. Just outside the school gates was one vast open space. Along one side of this space, directly opposite the school gates, rebuilding was taking place. Bricklayers, carpenters, plasterers, electricians and plumbers and indeed anyone else involved in the building all took their tea breaks at the same time, and this particular day this break coincided with my PE lesson.

During this tea break all the men, young and old, came to sit on or below the wall which surrounded the building site.

I was well prepared for the lesson. We were all just about to leave the classroom, all children wearing the required clothing; vest and shorts for the boys, vest and navy-blue knickers for the girls, plimsolls for everyone, carrying baskets of small balls, skipping ropes and hoops, when in walks a tutor from college. She had come to watch my lesson and write a report on my progress.

The lesson started well. The children were responsive and appeared to enjoy what they were doing. I was feeling quite confident and actually enjoying myself when one little boy threw his ball in the direction of the railings. It went through the railings and started to roll across the waste ground.

He immediately followed it through the gate, retrieved it and brought it back. Obviously I had to have a word with him and I told him that if his ball accidentally went through the railings again he was not, definitely not, to leave the playground by himself to retrieve it.

This message was obviously overheard by the rest of the class. The next moment, to my absolute horror, another handful of children deliberately threw their balls through the railings and proceeded to chase them across the waste ground. They appeared to be totally deaf to any calls I made for them to return immediately, and the only thing I could do was to run after them and, once I had caught up with them, herd them back through the gate.

Of course this was a cause of great amusement among the men sitting outside the building site who were enjoying their tea break. I think I can still hear the cheers, the whoops, the wolf whistles and the various comments and catcalls which filled the air as I, dressed in T-shirt and shorts, ran across the wasteland chasing little boys, most of whom were deliberately kicking their balls further away.

I eventually managed to round them all up and even managed to collect all the balls. I then proceeded to usher them back into the playground to a series of cheers, catcalls and wolf whistles from the watching crowd.

As I came into the playground and closed the big gate behind me, besides the humiliation I felt, I also had a terrible feeling that I would get a really bad write-up from the tutor who was at this moment watching every move. But when I plucked up the courage to look in her direction, I saw her leaning against the wall with tears rolling down her cheeks as she desperately tried to control her laughter.

As it turned out she thought I handled the situation well, that I was in control throughout and that my lesson was well thought out and well executed!

35

During that year I also completed practice at a school in Ashton-under-Lyne and also at Poundswick School in Wythenshawe.

I may already have mentioned that we, the students, were totally responsible for finding our own way to whichever school we were sent to. This involved travelling on buses – often more than one bus in order to reach our destination. Quite often these buses were already full, almost to capacity when we boarded them. Often it was standing room only.

I need to add that we would normally be carrying a lot of equipment. Bags of books, marked and ready to return to the children. Rolled-up charts, maps and pictures relating to whichever topic we were teaching at the time. Visual aids to help bring the lessons alive.

On one occasion I was waiting for the bus, carrying most of the aforementioned articles, including a visual aid for one of the lessons that day.

The lesson was about tadpoles and frogs. My visual aid consisted of an extremely large jam jar containing water, a small amount of pond weed and a large number of tadpoles. The top of the jar was covered with a metal lid which just clipped onto the rim. Holes had been punched into the lid to allow air to circulate. Everything else had been packed into bags which hung on my shoulders or around my neck, which left two hands free to carry the jar.

Unfortunately when my bus arrived it was standing room only. Not easy when you need two hands to hold the jar! At first all went well and we set off from Didsbury towards the centre of Manchester. Then it happened! Something, or someone, caused the bus driver to perform an emergency stop! This had a disastrous effect on the passengers.

Those lucky enough to be seated were able to brace themselves by placing their hands on the seat in front, whereas those standing were not quite so lucky. Most managed to grab hold of the side of one of the seats or to grab hold of a rail on the ceiling of the bus. If only it had been that simple for me!

Whereas everybody else was able in some way to control their sudden precipitation towards the front of the bus, no such luxury was available for me!

I pitched forward crashing into the person in front of me, the lid shot off the top of my glass jar and most of the contents of the jar proceeded to travel upwards and forwards, hitting people directly in front of me and landing on the floor. Sadly the tadpoles left the jar with the water and were now wriggling on the floor of the bus.

Scrabbling around on the floor of the bus I managed to retrieve the lid and desperately tried to scoop up wriggling tadpoles, whilst trying to apologise to people in front of me who were trying to dry off, probably still totally unaware of the small black wriggly creatures which were disappearing under their collars, or of pieces of pond weed decorating their jackets.

Totally at a loss as to what to do next and fully aware that many poor little tadpoles were about to die on the floor of a double-decker bus in Manchester because I was unable to reach them to save them, as well as being fully aware that people were now beginning to realise how wet they were and their anger was mounting by the second, I decided that discretion was the better part of valour and I jumped off the bus at the next stop. After all, water may not have been the only thing to land on them!

I will never know how many tadpoles died that day, or what the cleaners thought when they cleaned the bus that night, but I do know that when I looked at my jar whilst standing at the bus stop in the pouring rain – oh yes I forgot to say it had started raining by now – I do know that I had about one inch of water left and five tadpoles.

36

Besides the time spent in schools there was also a lot of hard work to be done regarding coursework. I was doing well with all my compulsory subjects, and I was happy with my English literature course. I was finding maths hard but I thought I was coping!

At the end of the first term Mr Cresswell set his maths groups an exam to see how we were getting on. A couple of days later I was in the queue for supper when I felt a hand on my shoulder. Turning, I looked up to see Mr Creswell, my maths tutor. "I think you and I need to have a little chat," he said. "Come to see me after supper."

We met after supper and he told me he was really concerned after marking my test. He offered to tutor me on my own until I caught up with the rest of the group. I think he was the best teacher I ever had in my whole life. Mathematics had always been a mystery to me.

Possibly because previous teachers had never bothered to explain. They just showed examples and said that is the way we do it. The presumption was that we understood. Mr Cresswell was different. All of a sudden, under his expert tuition, things began to fall into place.

All of a sudden methods of solving problems suddenly made sense because he had explained the process in a way that I could understand. He explained how, and he explained why.

Up until then my teachers had simply said, "Here is a problem, this is how you solve it." No explanations, no reasoning behind it. Mr Creswell revealed a new world entirely. Logic and reasoning meant that everything suddenly made sense and made you wonder why on earth you had not been able to see this before!

These tutorials continued throughout the year, and at the end of the year I entered the room to sit my maths examination with more confidence than in any other subjects.

When I received my teacher's certificate at the end of the two years I was grateful to all those who had helped me along the way, but I was especially grateful to the wonderful maths lecturer, his patience and his kindness.

Besides working hard, I think we also found time for relaxing. As already stated we kept up our membership with the rambling club and the climbing club.

Nobody had much money so most evenings were spent in the common room often playing cards.

Occasionally a serious game of three-card brag would take place and quite often Derek and I were simply spectators. As I have already said most of the male students had done national service and many of them were already extremely proficient at playing games like poker and brag. Money was scarce for all students and even though The Old Cock Inn was directly opposite the college, it was rarely frequented by students of the college back in the early '50s.

Now and again some of us might be found drinking coffee in the little café which was next to the pub.

Occasionally, after saving up for a few weeks, Derek and I were able to have a proper night out! Back then ten shillings would take us to the cinema just down the road in Didsbury Village, with seats upstairs. It would also buy ten Park Drive cigarettes, and afterwards we were able to have a sit-down supper in the small restaurant in the local fish and chip shop.

Occasionally we would catch a bus to take us down into Manchester where we would go to one of the university union dances. This was about the only place where I saw any of my friends actually drinking alcohol. Possibly it was a lot cheaper in the union bars.

It's hard to believe I know, but we rarely drank alcohol back then. Some weekends we would spend with Pat and his wife Nancy at their home in Hyde. These were always enjoyable times. Sometimes we would visit Derek's aunt Doris and his uncle Ernie. Always enjoyable. We always returned to college very well fed!

Money was always scarce. Occasionally we would receive letters from home with a very welcome pound note or even a ten-shilling note enclosed in the letter. I didn't realise it back then but on many occasions my mother must have gone without something herself in order to send money to me.

I remember on one occasion receiving a small weighty package from home. My mother had been saving silver three penny bits for many years but as she was unable to send money in any other form, she sent me the coins instead. I had to take them to the bank to exchange them for notes. I have no recollection of how much I received from them, but I do remember being so grateful.

Playing cards in the common room early on a Saturday evening became quite popular. After a while three card brag became the most popular game to be played.

Most of us steered clear of joining games where money was concerned, but eventually we noticed that couples and friends were joining in in order to try to make enough money to go out for the evening. It became quite a normal thing. Those that were successful and won the money pot were able to go out for the evening, whereas the rest stayed in or went for a walk.

The stakes were never high, nobody had much money. It was always very friendly and those who lost took it in good part.

After all, nobody could possibly lose very much. Derek and I often watched the game but on a couple of occasions we were persuaded to join in. We had played a couple of times and dropped out very early, but then came the game that I will never forget.

Derek dropped out early and I ended up with a prial of nines. Obviously I kept playing.

In the rules that we played by, those that had been set right at the beginning, the highest hand was a prial of threes, followed by a prial of nines, then aces, kings, queens and so on. I have since been told that three nines is not normally the second-highest hand in three-card brag, only in nine-card brag. However those were the rules we always played to so when I looked at my hand and saw three nines I couldn't quite believe it.

Obviously I kept playing; after all, in my mind there was only one hand that could beat it and it was highly unlikely that somebody was holding a prial of threes. So, I kept playing and eventually there were just two of us left in the game – myself and Brenda.

Derek was by this time sitting behind me fully aware of the cards I was holding. Like me he was convinced that this was a pot that we were going to win. Therefore when I ran out of money he added whatever money he had left in his pocket.

At the same time Ted had joined Brenda and he was doing the same by putting his money there for Brenda. I can't remember the actual detail of how the game ended, i.e. who saw who, but what I can remember is the moment when we turned over the cards and I revealed a prial of nines.

I felt confident, as there was only one hand that could beat it. When Brenda turned over her cards and revealed a prial of threes, everyone was in total disbelief!

The outcome was Ted and Brenda won all the money on the table and Derek and I were left penniless. I need to add that we never played cards in college again. There were those who said afterwards that the game was fixed in some way. I never wanted to believe that!

During that final year some of us helped to organise and to take part in a revue. One of the main organisers was Drusilla, Drew for short. Drew's personality and enthusiasm was enough to get us all involved.

I remember Derek performing a duet, partnered by another student whose name I forget. I do remember they were very good and the song they sang was 'Me and My Shadow'.

I was in the chorus. I think there were six of us. We were chosen because we could do the best 'high kicks'.

The first dance, choreographed by Drew, was to the music of 'Cleo and Meo', a song about a baby crocodile that lived on the Allegheny River near Pittsburgh.

Costumes consisted of a sheet tightly wrapped around our body, flat shoes and Cleopatra-style wigs.

She also choreographed a dance for us to the music of 'Singing in the Rain'. For this dance we wore one-piece swimsuits, high-heeled shoes and carried an umbrella.

We also made up background scenes for quite a few of the other acts.

I can't remember what we called the revue, but I know it was successful because of the tremendous applause we received and the many shouts of, "More" and "Encore"!

In February 1954, a Valentine's Day dance was organised at the college. Sadly, a couple of days before the dance, I was taken ill with a high temperature and developed a rash. I was immediately isolated in the sick bay. I remained in the sick bay for the next few days, and therefore missed the dance which I had been looking forward to.

The sick bay was located on the first floor, and I have memories on the night of the dance, of hearing something hit the window of the room I was in. I got out of bed, walked over to the window and looked down to see Derek looking up and holding a large red paper heart, which he had obviously taken from the many hearts decorating the hall.

I opened the window, and we talked for a long time. From time to time we were joined by other friends, all of whom were determined to let me know that I was missed from this very special Valentine dance!

37

All of a sudden the dreaded final examinations were looming!

We were nearing the end of our two very special years at Didsbury. Two years into which we had crammed so much. Now we were about to be tested on what we had learned in those two years.

All of a sudden this was serious. It was so important that I gained my certificate. My mother had sacrificed so much for me since the day I was born and I couldn't let her down.

So began a few weeks of intense learning, and in my case cramming. For days before each exam I worked long into the night revising and cramming as much knowledge as I could. And I wasn't alone.

Often as I went to make a cup of tea in the kitchen at about 2am I would meet other students doing exactly the same. Of course this cramming of knowledge was not necessary for everybody – Derek for example only needed to read through his notes. Knowledge that he had gained throughout his two years was already firmly established in his mind. He remembered everything… no need for cramming. And there were others like him.

I was always in awe of his intelligence and his ability to remember everything, seemingly without effort. I'm trying to remember the exams that we had. There were exams in the main subjects we had chosen to study. Mine were English literature and mathematics.

Then there were the compulsory subjects, such as English language, basic mathematics, psychology, teaching methods based on the years we had chosen to teach (mine was five to eleven years), classroom organisation and child development.

English literature was fine although it did mean reading a couple of the books that were on the list. Books that I had previously skimmed through. I also remember cramming lots and lots of quotations. Quotations from poetry, quotations from plays, quotations from novels. English language was fine. Basic maths was fine, however much work was needed (with the help of my saviour Mr Creswell) in my other specialist subject, mathematics.

Basic numeracy, simple algebra, and geometry I was fine with, but when it came to calculus, mechanics, and statistics I was in a nightmare world. As I said, had it not been for my wonderful maths tutor I wouldn't have stood a chance in hell.

Psychology was easy. After all there is no right or wrong approach, instead multiple perspectives are totally acceptable. Exams eventually were over and we were able to relax. Perhaps 'relax to a certain extent' was a little more correct for some of us.

The day right at the end of term – when we discovered our fate – eventually arrived and we were handed our certificates along with a letter from Mr Body the principal. The letter was in the form of a reference for future employers.

I almost cried with relief when I received my certificate for teaching. I had passed all my exams and the joy and relief was indescribable. Of course Derek passed as well, the difference being that he passed with distinctions in everything.

Derek and I had pondered long and hard as to what we were going to do at the end of the two years.

We had both decided that in fairness to our mothers who had both sacrificed much to allow us to go to college, we would return home, me to Darlington and Derek to Stockport, where we would work for a year before we married.

With this in mind we had already applied for teaching posts close to our own home. I applied to Darlington Education Authority and Derek applied to Manchester. I seem to remember that Derek was very quickly offered an appointment at a secondary school in Manchester.

Derek had done a couple of school practices at secondary schools and then he was sent to Poundswick Junior School. It was while he was there that he discovered that he absolutely loved teaching junior age children. Also the headmistress Miss Gladys Stevens loved him. She thought he was brilliant and I think she probably offered him a job on the spot. Derek turned down the secondary school offer and accepted an appointment at Poundswick Junior School.

As for me, I was offered an interview with Darlington Education Authority. I will never forget that interview.

When I arrived at the education offices I was asked to wait in a room along with about a dozen other extremely nervous young women. One by one we were called in for interview.

The scene before me as I walked into the interview room has stayed with me forever. The room was huge. It was dominated by a huge polished oak table which stretched across the width of the room. From the centre of that table another long oak table stretched almost the length of the room.

Around the huge table which stretched across the width of the room sat nine or even ten adults. At the end of the second table – the one which stretched the length of the room – was one solitary chair. When I entered the room that one solitary chair was the first thing I saw. My eyes then travelled the length of the long table. I then saw the adults who were sitting staring at me. No one was smiling. Those who were wearing spectacles were looking at me over the top of their spectacles. I stood there feeling a mixture of bewilderment and panic. I then heard a voice say, "Please sit!" So I sat.

After what seemed an eternity of answering questions which were barked at me from all directions, I was eventually told that I could leave and that I would be contacted. As I left I realised why all the people who had exited the room before me looked so nervous!

In Darlington you are employed by the authority and then allocated to any school they choose to send you to!

Two or three weeks later I received a letter telling me that I had been successful in my application and was given a date in September to attend a newly built school in the town where I was to start my first teaching post on the day it opened.

But back to the final weeks of college. A mixture of feelings pervaded. It was exciting to be starting a totally new chapter in our lives, but it was tinged with sadness that we were going to leave people we had spent the last two years with.

At that time Didsbury College was in its infancy and the number of students was quite small. Therefore we knew every single student who was there in the years 1952 to 1954. We had made special friendships with so many of them and no one realised that apart from keeping in touch by letters, it was likely that we may never meet some of them again. As it happens that turned out to be so true. Apart from Helen who lived in Darlington, and Patrick and Geoff who lived locally in Manchester or the surrounding area, I don't think I ever met one single person ever again.

Everything was packed up, my cabin trunk was picked up and somehow it returned safely home to 37 Greenbank Road, Darlington where it was carried to our huge attic room and left there.

We had left college, we had our new jobs waiting for us in September, and we had the whole summer ahead of us to do whatever we pleased. We had decided that we would love to visit Scotland again, but we had very little money. We didn't have enough time to take summer jobs in order to pay for a holiday such as the one we had had the previous year.

Shortly after we left college for the last time, Derek cycled once more over the Pennines and came to stay at Greenbank Road. The first thing he did was to persuade me to take my beautiful Royal Enfield bicycle down to the cycle shop where after a lot of bartering I exchanged it for a sleek racing bike.

Derek had this wonderful idea that we could cycle to Scotland, tour the lowlands of Scotland and stay in youth hostels. He had saved enough money for us to be able to do that. I still have the suspicion that the money came from Aunties Flo and Doris.

Hence about a week later, when I'd had time to get used to the bike, we set off. When I say 'get used to the bike', I suppose I mean I had to get used to a whole different experience.

On my Royal Enfield bicycle I had the most comfortable seat to sit on. It was soft and it was well sprung. Now I had a hard, rigid, most uncomfortable strip of solid leather.

On my Royal Enfield bicycle I could steer whilst still maintaining a comfortable position… sitting on my comfortable seat!

Now in order to be able to steer and to reach the brakes, I had to lean forward until I was almost horizontal, with my chin almost resting on the handlebars and my head tilted upwards in a most uncomfortable position in order to be able to see where I was going.

In other words comfort was a thing of the past.

There was also a set of gears, eight in total. I found it really difficult to change gear… I was never really sure which gear I was supposed to be in anyway! Nevertheless we prepared for the holiday.

Shorts, appropriate shoes, a waterproof jacket, and a cycling cape were essential. Also packed into limited space in a small bag which was fixed behind the saddle, we carried necessary toiletries, clean underwear and socks, a warm sweater and a couple of clean tops (T-shirts for girls were not yet fashionable) and a clean pair of shorts.

We left Darlington early one morning heading for Carlisle. A distance back then at a guess would be about eighty miles. I do not remember the exact route we took. Derek had planned it in detail and back then in the '50s there were no motorways to be avoided and not nearly as much traffic as today.

It soon became obvious that the hills were going to be a problem for me. Cycling up them that is… I was okay coming down! After a while we agreed that Derek would cycle up them and wait for me at the top. That was my decision not his! On one occasion I had dismounted and was beginning to push my bike up a very steep hill. It began to rain quite heavily so I unpacked my cycling cape and in doing so somehow managed to drop the pump – my shiny new pump, from my shiny new bicycle. As I watched it roll across the road a car approached. I frantically tried to point to my bicycle pump but the driver totally ignored me and proceeded to run right over my pump which shattered into many pieces. One of the very few cars that had so far passed me. I remember I was really upset, so much so I think I actually jumped up and down and screamed at the car.

Looking back it's very difficult to believe how much times have changed. Back in the '50s it was possible for us to enjoy cycling across the Pennines without fearing for our lives. Over miles we would encounter a handful of cars, a few lorries, two or three motorbikes and quite a few horse-drawn farmers carts. I can't remember how far we managed to travel that day.

Eighty miles was so easy for Derek but much more difficult for someone like me. I have a feeling we probably reached Brough or Penrith and stayed in a hostel there.

Youth hostels were great places to stay and I have already told stories of holidays in my teens which included hostels, however in the past I had travelled with girlfriends where we were able to stay in the same dormitory.

This time it was different. Derek had to stay in the men's dormitory and I had to stay in the girl's dormitory. Times are different now. They have mixed dormitories. I suppose they would find it extremely difficult to ask people to conform to the rules we had back then.

However, back to our cycling trip. The following day we had breakfast together (we were allowed to do that!), then we set off for Carlisle.

I really can't remember the hostels that we stayed in – it is so long ago – but I know that after Carlisle we headed for the Trossachs, and we stayed in a lot of heavily wooded areas. I also remember the sheer beauty of the countryside.

Days were tiring but extremely satisfying, and the evenings were usually entertaining as we met other travellers in the hostels and shared our experiences. One of the people we met was named Duncan. He was Scottish and originated from the outskirts of Glasgow. Duncan was working as a forester and was just enjoying a holiday exploring the beautiful countryside close to his home.

The three of us became good friends and for the next few days Duncan travelled with us wherever we went. He showed us places we would not have found without him. I was quite happy, because now when we were going uphill I had company.

Unlike Derek, who seemed to be able to travel up the steepest hill without any problems at all, Duncan, like me, needed to get off and push his bike.

After a few days of travelling around I think Duncan mentioned the fact that he had never been to England and that one day he would love to visit the Lake District. Guess what? The next thing I remember is us heading south towards the beautiful Lake District.

We spent quite a few days travelling around and visiting various hostels in and around the Lake District. I remember it was breathtakingly beautiful. After a while a pattern emerged.

At the bottom of each hill… and believe me there were lots of hills!

(In fact looking back I remember pushing my bike up hills, and I remember the exhilarating ride down the other side freewheeling all the way but I don't remember many 'flat bits'.)

Anyway back to what I was saying, at the bottom of each hill Duncan and I would dismount whilst Derek shot off into the distance, and we would walk slowly up the hill. We would meet up with Derek at the top, then we would all sit and chat before mounting our bikes again for the exhilarating ride down the other side.

After a few days, possibly a week, in the Lake District it was decided for some reason that we would continue to North Wales. I do remember Duncan asking if it was as hilly in North Wales as it was in the Lake District. I do recall Derek telling him that North Wales was as flat as a pancake! The next thing I remember was that we were on our way to North Wales.

I have absolutely no recollection as to how we got there, but I do remember cycling along somewhere near Rhyll on the North Wales coast when Duncan said to me, "I hope you don't mind me saying but you have some very funny pancakes in Wales. This is certainly not flat!" Derek and I both laughed.

The rest of the holiday is a bit hazy. I remember saying goodbye to Duncan as we parted company somewhere near Northwich. He was travelling back to Scotland and we were heading for Stockport for a few days. After a few days in Stockport, Derek and I set off for Darlington. I remember parts of the journey, such as travelling down into Holmfirth.

Travelling down such steep hills that I feared my brakes might not work.

Thankfully we reached Darlington eventually and I think Derek stayed for a couple of days. Then it was time to say goodbye for a while. A time we had been dreading, but one that we knew had to come. I was to stay in Darlington and take up my new teaching post. Derek had to travel back to Manchester to do the same. I was sad as I waved him off and knew it would be a couple of days at least before I knew he was home safely.

How easy it is these days… a quick phone call or even a text and we know immediately whether our loved ones have arrived safely at their destination. Of course more well-off families had telephones but we didn't, and Derek's family also didn't, so it was a matter of waiting for the post.

A post which for the next twelve months would deliver letters on alternate days to 37 Greenbank Road, Darlington and to 12 Dorset Avenue, Cheadle Hume. Then it was down to preparation for a new job – my first real job and the realisation suddenly dawned on me. This was it… this was really it.

In a couple of weeks I had to walk into a class of children for whom I would be totally responsible and I was terrified at the thought of it. However, I comforted myself with the thought that I ought to be able to do the job and to do it well.

After all, a few weeks previously who would have thought that I would be able to cycle from Darlington to the Trossachs in Scotland, from there to the Lake District, then down to North Wales along the coast as far as Colwyn Bay or

Llandudno (I can't remember which), then back to Stockport and finally to Darlington across the Pennines?

If I could achieve that I should be able to achieve anything, at least that is what I hoped!

38

Sometime during that long summer break I visited my mother's dear friend Nell Stephenson. At this point in time it is getting more difficult to record things exactly. I can vividly remember the events but putting them into an exact time slot is becoming more difficult (I think this happened before my never-to-be-forgotten cycling holiday).

I went to see Mrs Stephenson to talk to her all about my forthcoming marriage, about my husband-to-be Derek, and about my appointment as an infant teacher at a school in Darlington. In fact a total catch-up on everything. Notice I still refer to her as Mrs Stephenson.

When I was a child things were much more formal than today. We children referred to adults by their formal title, Mr or Mrs. Either that or we called them Auntie or Uncle, even though they were not related in any way.

It was considered impolite to address an adult by their first name, thus they became aunties and uncles, or received their full title of Mr or Mrs Whoever! But back to my story…

When I told Mrs Stephenson about my appointment she was very excited. Excited because only three doors away she had new neighbours.

Her new neighbour had been appointed as headmaster of my new school. She insisted that I called and introduced myself to him. This was the last thing I wanted to do but Mrs Stephenson was convinced that it would be the right thing to do as it would show that I was keen and interested in my work.

I do remember the feeling of being confronted with a totally impossible situation. On the one hand I was being advised to do something by someone who was very dear to me, someone who had my best interests at heart throughout the whole of my life, and who was convinced she was advising me to do the right thing, yet on the other hand, I had a feeling that this was entirely the wrong thing to do. Nevertheless I allowed myself to be persuaded to knock on the door of the man who was to be my new headmaster.

I can remember the apprehension I felt as I opened the garden gate, walked up the garden path and knocked on the door. Had I not known that Mrs Stephenson was watching me, I think I would have fled. I know now, as I knew then, that that would have been the best course of action… but I didn't run. The door was opened by the man himself. He wasn't particularly tall, middle-aged with very white hair and a white moustache.

I introduced myself and I was invited in. I was taken into the front room, was given a cup of tea, and was made to feel most welcome. We talked for quite a while. To this day I've no idea what we talked about. I do remember him telling me that he intended to write to all the new staff to invite us to meet before the school term began.

I remember when I left he appeared to be extremely friendly, he was smiling and saying that he looked forward to the start of the new term. So how was it then that I knew that I had really done the wrong thing? I know that I had pleased Mrs Stephenson, but deep down I knew that I had not done myself any good at all.

I think I learned a lesson that day and that was: never allow yourself to be talked into anything that you know is wrong simply because you are afraid of hurting someone's feelings. Strange to say I never did receive a letter for the meeting that was held before the term began, though everybody else did!

The first I knew about it was when I turned up at school on the day before the term started, following instructions in a letter sent from the education committee. I discovered that the rest of the staff had received a letter from the headmaster and had all met a couple of weeks previously. When I explained that I had never received a letter, the secretary was very apologetic. She couldn't understand how this had happened.

The headmaster just smiled and said, "Don't worry, these things happen!" But it was the way he smiled! I was shown to my classroom – the classroom where I was to spend the next year of my life.

When we were talking in his house he had asked me which age group I preferred and also if there was an age group I particularly wanted to avoid. I told him that I liked top infants and that I was not particularly happy with reception class. Guess what I had… reception class!

Everything in the classroom was brand new. It was furnished with fifteen rectangular tables each with two small chairs. Around the sides of the room were bookshelves heaped with brand-new books of all shapes and sizes. There were shelves of plastic trays containing building bricks, jigsaw puzzles, crayons, paint pots, in fact everything that was needed.

Everything was new and unspoiled and for that first day I was in heaven. I was able to arrange the room in the way that I wanted to.

Unlike the classrooms in which I had completed my many school practices – classrooms in Victorian buildings with windows so high that you could only see the sky – this was a brand-new school and the windows covered the whole of one side of the classroom with views out across playing fields. Also a door led out of the classroom onto an outside space with water troughs and sand trays. As I have already said, it was heaven.

Besides preparing my classroom I was also able to explore the school. The hall was large, airy and full of sunlight, and equipped with all the latest PE equipment including frames attached to the wall, many of which could be swung out from the wall to make climbing frames.

I also met the rest of the staff. The head of the infant department was called Mrs Cook. She was delightful. Extremely friendly, always ready to help and to give advice and one of the best infant teachers I have ever met. She had the top infant class.

Next door to me with middle infants was a girl I knew from school! An extremely attractive girl called Isabel – I couldn't believe it. Isabel, like Helen, had been in the year above me at school. I also knew that at that time she was going out with a boy I knew called Colin.

The rest of the staff were really friendly and I began to look forward to my first year.

The following day when I arrived at school I really did have butterflies in my stomach. This was the day that new entrants were to be admitted to the school. We were dispatched to our classrooms and told to await our pupils. As parents came to the school and registered their children they were to be sent to the appropriate classroom. It might be useful to point out that in those days there were no such things as infant helps or assistant teachers – it was down to you, and you alone.

That first day was a day never to be forgotten. Having registered the children, parents would bring them to my classroom and attempt to leave them. When I say attempt, it could be because the children were tearful and didn't want to leave their mothers, or it could be that the mothers were tearful and didn't want to leave the children.

I did my best to occupy each and every one of them, and to console and comfort those who were distressed. When we reached the number of thirty I truly thought that that was my class, after all there were only thirty chairs. However, whoever had calculated the number of children to be registered at that school on that day was way out – I ended up with forty-six children!

Some were crying for their mothers; two of them actually screaming because their mothers had left them. Some arguing about the fact that they had chosen a piece of equipment first and someone else was trying to take it from them. It was in fact total chaos and it was up to me and me alone to sort it out! It was no good expecting any help from my colleagues as they were experiencing the same pressures that I was.

Somehow, by some miracle that to this day cannot be explained, I managed to occupy each and every child, and also to send forty-six children safely home at the end of the day. I also remember that what made it all worthwhile were the hugs that I had from the children as they said goodbye to me and went home with their parents.

Over the next few days adjustments were made to cater for the number of children who had registered at the school. I ended up with over forty children and they each had a chair! I soon realised that organisation was key to success and the children were delightful.

I was fortunate that in that year I didn't have any particularly disruptive children, though many of them had very strong personalities. I came to love them all.

The children absolutely loved PE lessons, especially when we used the big apparatus in the hall. I enjoyed these lessons also because now I did not have to dress up in T-shirt and shorts.

However, I soon discovered that giving them free rein did not work well – mainly because there were so many children in the class and also because some activities were more popular than others. Therefore just to allow them to choose where to go always ended up with over half the class being on one particular piece of apparatus. The best way to organise them was to have a number of teams. The number of teams depended on the number of different activities taking place on different pieces of apparatus. After a set amount of time on each piece of apparatus, I would stop them and they would move on to the next piece. This made sure that every child had the opportunity to enjoy every activity.

On one occasion we had HMIs (Her Majesty's Inspectors) in school. One of them decided to visit my PE lesson. The children were brilliant – nobody misbehaved and nobody showed off.

However, the inspector decided that she didn't like what she was seeing and said to me that it was, "far too organised", and did I realise that "children were capable of sorting themselves out" and would "use their common sense and go and find another place to play".

She told me that I was underestimating their intelligence and that we needed to allow children to make their own mistakes. She advocated that I gave free rein to the class. She told me that they would soon sort out what to do and that I would discover that they would not at any time overcrowd any one piece of apparatus.

I think I thought that, as I was being spoken to as if I was an idiot, I would pretend to be one. I told her that I could not quite understand what she meant so could she please show me.

She was delighted to be asked. She called all the children to sit around her. She then proceeded to give them a small talk on how they should use the various pieces of apparatus, and how they should be aware that if there were too many people on the apparatus, they were to go and find somewhere else to play. Then with a very smug expression she told me to watch just how sensible they all were. She then told them to go and choose where they wanted to be.

They stood up. They turned… and they ran. They ran (with few exceptions) to the favourite piece of apparatus… the one with the slide.

I think I managed to keep the smile off my face as I watched her smug expression change to one of panic as she attempted to pull almost forty children off the slide.

At the end of the week each inspector handed in their reports with comments about each member of staff and the lessons they had watched and advised on. Strangely enough no comment was made about my PE lesson.

However, another of the inspectors who sat in with me for a whole morning, a morning in which we ended up with the whole class taking part in number rhymes, gave me an absolutely glowing report. She said she had rarely seen a class of such young children so totally absorbed in what they were doing.

We were all expected to eat lunch at school. The headmaster said that if it was good enough for the children it was good enough for the staff. We all sat together at one table at the end of the dining room. Besides the headmaster there were seven members of the teaching staff in total: three in the infant department and four in the junior department.

Conversations between members of staff were normally dominated by the headmaster. He was quite domineering and certainly enjoyed his role. I purposely avoided involvement in conversation unless I had to speak.

One day a member of the junior staff discovered that I had attended Didsbury College. He knew somebody who had been there and was chatting to me about my time at the college. Isabel and Mrs Cook both knew that I was engaged to be married, but as it had never come up in conversation before, the rest of the staff were not aware. When they found out they were all really interested and offered congratulations. Many wanted to know when the wedding would take place and for a moment it was a very happy conversation.

However, our headmaster had a very different opinion. I can still remember his reaction. "What," he said in a loud voice, loud enough for nearby children to hear. "Engaged? You should have had your bottom smacked!" Nobody said a word, and what had been a friendly animated discussion with a lot of smiles suddenly became a deadly silence.

Strangely enough back in the '50s we accepted being spoken to like that. These days I think it would be quite different. Looking back he was known for speaking to people as though they were children. I remember one occasion, I think it was a bank holiday, but it could have been a weekend, the whole of the staff gave up a day to take the fourth years on a trip to the seaside.

We had a wonderful day. We all did our bit to ensure that the children had a great time. We arranged team games, we built sandcastles, we ended with a game of rounders which gave the children great pleasure, and also entertained many other people who were on the beach, some of whom joined in and helped to field the ball. It was a happy group, children and staff, who boarded the coach to take us home.

The next day at school, before school started, we were all summoned to the headmaster's office. Once inside we stood in front of his desk, a bit like naughty children, whilst he reprimanded us. Evidently he found the whole day disorganised and our behaviour totally unacceptable. He refused to allow anybody to speak in their own defence and just shouted at us, a bit like a sergeant on a parade ground. We were dismissed with the warning that if we did not improve our ways, there would be consequences!

It was obviously his way of trying to humiliate us, particularly his two male teachers. Both male teachers were particularly good teachers, popular with pupils, parents and staff alike.

Thankfully it would be many years, decades even, before I encountered such a bully of a headteacher again. I have been really fortunate that during my career I have worked for good people who are good at their job and kind and considerate to the staff.

At the end of the term I was sorry to leave the children. I had become very fond of all of them. I was sorry to leave the staff as I had made new friends.

Before I left, the staff presented me with the gift of a clock as a wedding present. Mrs Cook told me that, as head of the infant department, she had requested that she wrote my reference at the end of my first year which was my probationary year. She showed me a copy and what she had written was very fair.

39

The year had been very busy for me in other ways as well. Derek and I corresponded by letter every other day for the whole year. We certainly kept the postman busy! We managed to get together at Christmas and Easter for a short period. But I had something really important to plan… my wedding!

Fortunately weddings in the early '50s were reasonably simple affairs. Thank goodness they didn't cost the tens of thousands of pounds people pay these days. It was a good job they didn't as I had no money. Derek had no money, and my mother certainly had no money.

In those days, it was the bride's parents who were expected to foot the bill for everything. My mother was brilliant. She was determined that I was going to have the perfect wedding. First thing to book was the church… after we fixed a date of course.

We discovered that the church was free on Saturday 6th August. It was my church, the church I had attended throughout all my teenage years. Holy Trinity Church, Woodland Road, Darlington.

One of the first things Derek and I had to do was to visit the vicar who would conduct the ceremony. Many changes had taken place during the two years I spent at Didsbury College. The vicar who had run the church for the past few years had become ill. He had mental health problems, which back then were rarely recognised, and he sadly ended up taking his own life. Obviously until the new vicar could be appointed, people helped out from other churches.

We were extremely fortunate to be paired with the Reverend LP Griffin to conduct our service. We had never met him before, so we were both extremely apprehensive as we turned up at his house, as requested, to discuss the solemnity of the vows we were about to undertake.

It was immediately after we met him that we knew how lucky we were. I think he was one of the nicest vicars that I had ever met. As I said we were both very nervous, but he soon put us at our ease. I remember sitting there, listening to him speak. The only sound in the room was his voice.

Suddenly a rumbling sound filled the room! The rumbling sound became louder and I looked at Derek who had gone very red in the face. I then realised that the rumbling sound was coming from Derek's tummy. There was nothing he could do to stop it and I realised that the red face was pure embarrassment.

I think I have already said that if something strikes me as funny, there is nothing I can do to stop myself from laughing. The solemnity of this occasion made no difference. I dissolved into fits of giggles. I remember looking at the Reverend Griffin and to my immense relief, he was laughing as well. Yes I felt sorry for Derek but there was nothing I could do.

Shortly after that, Reverend Griffin's wife supplied us with tea and home-made cake. I am sure this helped with

Derek's gurgling problems. We talked for a long time, not just about our vows, but about all sorts of things. At the end of the meeting Reverend Griffin told us that, having met us, he was confident that we would have a long and successful marriage.

We also had a meeting with the organist. We chose Mendelssohn to be played when I entered the church. Derek had a great love of Wagner's music and he requested a selection to be played as people were entering the church, and whilst they were sitting waiting for the ceremony to begin.

I can't list the actual pieces of music played, I just remember it was quite rousing, and I remember that the organist commented that he had never been asked to play that at a wedding before. One of the hymns we chose was 'Love Divine, All Loves Excelling'.

The wedding ceremony was booked for 2pm so my mother booked Grainger's Café on Northgate directly after the ceremony. I have no recollection of the food that was served, but I recently found a seating plan. The top table consisted of Derek and myself, my mother, my Uncle Rob (who was to give me away,) Derek's mother and Fred. My two bridesmaids were Anne and Sheila. Derek's best man was Pat, the groomsmen, George and Don, and my Auntie Hilda. Including those sitting at the top table, the number of people totalled sixty-three.

My mother also arranged the provision of the most beautiful three-tier wedding cake. I don't know how much the cake cost, but I do know that the whole reception amounted to a few pounds.

I was in charge of my wedding dress. It was still too soon after the war to be able to find an affordable wedding dress in the local shops or department stores. Therefore I did what most people did back then; I found a good dressmaker and I searched out a pattern. I remember I bought the pattern at Binns department store on the High Row. It was a Vogue pattern and to me it looked like a fairy-tale dress.

The materials used were satin and lace and I bought them locally, again at a shop on High Row, Darlington called Luck and Sons. I also chose a veil which Luck and Sons said they would keep for me until the time of my wedding.

I chose patterns for my two bridesmaid dresses and bought the material for them at the same time. The material was a beautiful shade between pink and lilac, in a soft, silky material. The dress was complimented by a velvet ribbon in a deeper, pinky lilac shade, which tied round the waist and hung down the front of the dress. I think Sheila made her own dress, and I can't remember if Anne did the same, or whether she went to a dressmaker.

We ordered the flowers, again locally. I knew I wanted lily of the valley in my bouquet. We ordered posies for the two bridesmaids, sprays for our mothers and buttonholes for Derek, for my Uncle Rob, for the best man and for the two groomsmen. So that was the church, the music in church, the reception, the cake, my dress, bridesmaids' dresses, and the flowers.

I remember my mother and I making a couple of extremely enjoyable trips to Newcastle to buy her outfit, and my trousseau. I wonder if the word trousseau is used anymore.

Back in the '50s all brides had a trousseau. It simply meant a collection of everything that we were going to need for our wedding (and for the honeymoon) in terms of clothing and accessories, including something borrowed, something blue, something old, and something new.

We were happy. We laughed a lot. Looking back I realise that my mother must have had mixed feelings. After all, after the wedding, I would be leaving home for good and moving to the other side of the country. She must have been quite sad at the thought of me moving away, but she never said a word.

One other thing that my mother organised was the photographer. At work, my mother had made friends with a lady called Mrs Doris Clifford. She was the personal secretary to the 'boss'. Mrs Clifford's daughter and her friend ran a photography business in the town, and they agreed to take the photographs at the wedding.

One occasion when laughter got the better of us was when my mother and I went shopping to buy shoes. We were in Newcastle and we were coming to the end of a very tiring day.

The previous week we had been to the cinema to see a film called *Arsenic and Old Lace*. A film about two sweet old ladies, who made a habit of murdering people and burying them in the cellar. As we sat in the shoe shop patiently waiting to be served, the shop door opened and in walked two very old ladies.

They both had very grey, almost white, hair. One had her hair fastened back into a bun at the back of her head, and the other had her hair piled up on top of her head also in a bun. They wore long fitted coats with the collars turned up at the back and lapels folded back, each one showing a high-necked blouse with ruffles fastened with a brooch. They were also wearing shiny black leather lace-up boots. They looked exactly like the two old ladies in the film!

My mother and I looked at one another and, in almost in the same breath, whispered the words, *Arsenic and Old Lace*. That was it. We just started to laugh and the more we tried to stop the more we laughed. When it was our turn to be served, and the shop assistant came to ask us what we would like to see, neither one of us could answer. We just laughed and laughed, and were completely unable to speak, even one word!

Our behaviour was disgraceful, unforgivable in fact, but we were totally unable to control ourselves. In the end, we decided that discretion was the better part of valour and left, almost bowing our way out of the shop whilst attempting to apologise profusely. I will never know what they made of us in that shop. All I know is that we eventually managed to get ourselves onto the train, still laughing and unable to hold a coherent conversation with anybody. I will never know why we thought it so funny. I suppose when hysteria sets in you can't really do anything about it!

After many trips to the dressmaker for fittings and more trips to Newcastle for more shopping, everything was ready and organised. Now it was just a matter of waiting for the big day. Waiting with a mixture of great excitement, and nerves… after all, there may have been something we had forgotten!

40

I am unable to remember the exact date on which we broke up for the summer holidays back in 1952. By then most arrangements had been made for the wedding on the 6th of August. Invitations had been sent out and all had been replied to. An invitation had been sent to my father. Evidently my mother considered it her duty to let him know that I was to be married.

I vividly remember coming home from work one day and discovering that a parcel had been delivered to me. My grandmother had taken delivery of the parcel. Shortly afterwards, my mother arrived home from work. She found me sitting at the kitchen table in floods of tears, with the opened parcel in front of me. I was holding a letter.

I don't to this day know why I was so upset, but it was probably because this was the first letter I had ever received from my father, and I was twenty years old!

In all those twenty years, there was never a birthday card, a Christmas card, a birthday gift, a Christmas gift or a letter of any kind. Now, here, in my hand, in his own handwriting, was a letter from my father, and in the box was a gift of a China tea set. First letter, first gift!

The letter was quite short, and in it he said because of the circumstances he had felt that it was better for everyone concerned that he left me totally in the care of my mother. He stated that throughout all those years, he had never forgotten me, and that he would like me to accept the gift of a tea set. After all these years, I was supposed to believe this?

I still don't know why I was so upset. Possibly I was angry! I certainly had no feelings for him. To this day, I have no feelings for him!

Strangely enough, I still have the tea set, almost complete. I think one cup was broken a long time ago. It's ironic to think that the set totalled twenty-one pieces. Six cups, six saucers, six plates, one milk jug, one sugar bowl and one large plate. One piece for every year of my life up till then, plus one!

My mother and I dealt with the situation as we always did back then. We made a cup of tea and sat and talked. Very soon I was laughing again and looking forward to getting on with my life.

Still to be organised was where to accommodate guests who were travelling from afar. I think we arranged for Derek's mum and Fred to stay with my Uncle Charlie and my Auntie Enid.

Doris, Ernie and Auntie Flo were to stay with my Uncle Rob and Auntie Mary. Also travelling from Stockport were Mr and Mrs Lacking, neighbours of Derek's mum, and their daughter and son-in-law. I can't remember where they stayed but I know everybody was well looked after.

Derek booked rooms at the Kings Head hotel, Darlington, for himself, Patrick, his best man, and for his groomsmen, Don and George. Nancy, Patrick's wife, was to stay with my

Uncle Rob. Other people who were travelling from afar made their own arrangements for accommodation.

All that remained for me to do was to have a final fitting for my dress, pick up my veil from Luck and Sons, and pack my suitcase for the honeymoon.

Suddenly the wedding was almost upon us. Relatives and friends from Stockport were met at the station and taken to wherever it was they were going to stay the night. I remember our neighbour Mr Saint was extremely busy with his taxi.

Derek, his best man Pat and his wife Nancy, and his groomsmen Don and George, arrived by train and went straight to the Kings Head hotel. Nancy was taken to stay with my Uncle Rob.

Hen nights were unheard-of back then, so no great parties were held in the days leading up to the wedding, by me or by my friends. However, stag nights were held, usually the night before the wedding. Derek was no exception. He, Pat, Don and George, once established in the Kings Head hotel, enjoyed a very liquid evening.

It was weeks, possibly months, later that the full story of what happened that night was told. It seemed that the four of them sat round a table in the lounge of the hotel and ordered drinks which were brought to them by a very amenable wine waiter. As the evening progressed and more drinks were ordered, the wine waiter was included, in other words, every time Derek and his friends had a drink, so did the wine waiter!

Quite late into the evening, possibly in the early hours, the wine waiter was asked to bring another round of drinks. By this time, Derek and his friends had moved from the lounge to a small snug, located one level down. This meant that the wine waiter had to negotiate a long flight of stairs. As they sat waiting for the last order to be delivered, they heard a tremendous crash. They all rushed, I think I ought to say staggered, out of the small snug to see what had happened. At the bottom of the stairs lay the wine waiter still clutching his tray and one glass minus most of its contents. The rest of the glasses and their contents were deposited all the way down the staircase.

I think what happened next was a bit of a blur to everyone, but somehow they managed to look after the waiter, help to clear up and get themselves to bed.

Whilst all this was going on my mother and I were finishing off preparations for the big day. The house had already had a big spring clean. Everything looked perfect. We finished off making up beds in my mother's bedroom and my bedroom in case unexpected guests arrived.

That night I had a long soak in the bath and washed my hair, my hair was quite long back then. Visits to the hairdresser were unheard-of. I had only once visited the hairdresser in my life. I can't remember exactly when, but I know I came home with an urchin cut! I think it broke my mother's heart.

I vividly remember that last evening. I remember sharing a bed with my mother in the spare bedroom and talking long into the night. I think that was when I realised how much she was going to miss me, and indeed how much I was going to miss her.

41

The day of my wedding arrived. We were up early. There was still quite a lot to do. Then quite unexpectedly there was a knock on the front door. I answered it and was very surprised to see Don and George standing there.

To this day, I have no idea why they thought that it was the correct thing for them to do. Why they thought the groomsmen to the groom should spend the morning with the bride-to-be! But what could I do? I invited them in and made them a cup of tea. It was always tea, never coffee in those days. They were already dressed in their suits, looking very smart, even though the wedding was not taking place for hours! I found out later that Derek had no idea where they had gone, and was praying that they would turn up at the church.

They slowly drank their tea and seated themselves in the living room at the back of the house. We had actually closed off the front sitting room as it had been prepared for any festivities that would happen later in the day. However, George didn't ever sit on a chair! He sprawled, he lolled, and he slouched horizontally with his extremely long legs stretched out in front of him as far as possible. This meant that every time anybody needed to pass from the kitchen, through the living room to access any other parts of the house, they had to step over George!

There were still many last-minute things to see to, after which my grandmother, my mother and myself needed time to bathe, dress and get ready for one of the most important days of my life. I remember that after one occasion when I tripped over George's legs, my patience came to an end and I became quite cross!

I vaguely remember suggesting that they went for a walk somewhere, anywhere, where they would be out of my way. I can still remember the expressions on their faces as they looked at one another, both probably thinking the same thing, "Poor Derek!" Anyway, whatever they were thinking it didn't matter to me. I just wanted them out of the way. I have no idea where they went, or how they spent their time, I didn't really care.

My mother, my grandmother and I were able to relax. I think we relaxed with a cup of tea and then we were able to think about getting ourselves ready.

My grandmother always liked to dress smartly, and on this particular day, she looked incredibly smart.

My mother, my dear dear mother, I had never seen her look more beautiful. She wore a two-piece suit with a pleated skirt in an incredibly beautiful shade of pale blue, a hat, bag and gloves and smart shoes completed the outfit. My Uncle Rob arrived on time, actually in plenty of time. He was always totally reliable.

The time came for me to put on my dress. I remember my mother zipping me into it. The last thing was to put on the headband and my veil. Back then I wore my hair quite long and it was very thick. Newly washed, it was also very springy and I remember it was no easy task to fix.

However, at last I was ready and I remember walking down the stairs and seeing my Uncle Rob, waiting for me at the bottom. He had tears in his eyes!

The time came for my mother and grandmother to leave for the church. That left Uncle Rob and myself alone and waiting for the taxi to return to pick us up. It's a good job my Uncle Rob had had three daughters – he was prepared for anything.

He even coped with a very nervous bride suddenly deciding that she needed to use the toilet. This meant going back upstairs and it meant him helping me to cope with the copious yards of material in the train of my wedding dress, whilst averting his eyes to save me any embarrassment.

At last, I was ready, the taxi came back and we climbed into it. It was actually only a few hundred yards to the church, so the journey was quite short.

When we arrived, I could see Sheila and Anne waiting for me in the porch. Also waiting were the photographers. Everyone else was inside the church. At least I hoped they were.

My uncle and I walked up the small slope towards the church porch. I remember it was quite breezy and all I could think about was that my veil was going to take off in the wind. However, we covered the small distance to the church and were soon safely in the porch.

Sheila and Anne busied themselves, straightening my veil, and spreading out the train to my wedding dress. The train was quite long.

One of the churchwardens was busy sending signals to those waiting at the altar that I had arrived. The rousing music being played by the organist suddenly ceased. There was a moment's silence, and then the organist started playing Mendelssohn's 'Wedding March'. My uncle offered me his arm, and we began the long slow walk down the aisle.

We were followed by my bridesmaids, Ann (who was actually my matron of honour) and Sheila. They were accompanied by Don and George, who miraculously had found their way to the church and actually shown everybody to their seats.

Fortunately, in 1955, we still did things the British way. American customs and habits had still not found their way into our ceremonies. Hence, my bridesmaids followed me, they did not precede me.

The church appeared to be full. I was too nervous to really notice individual faces as they turned and smiled as we proceeded down the aisle. I remember thinking that the church aisle was twice as long as I remembered it. Waiting at the end of the aisle in what seemed to be the far distance was Derek accompanied by his best man, Pat, and facing me was the Reverend Griffin.

We reached the front of the church. In the front pew to my left I briefly saw my mother shortly to be joined by my Uncle Rob. I was aware that in the front pew to my right was Derek's mother and her husband, Fred.

My attention, however, was fixed on my husband-to-be. He was smiling, though he did look as nervous as I felt. He looked handsome in his smart grey suit. Patrick his best man stood beside, but slightly behind, him and the Reverend

Griffin was looking straight at me with the most beautiful smile on his face.

He began by welcoming everybody on that day to this very special occasion, and we followed with the usual Church of England ceremony practised at all weddings.

Like most people in that time, we omitted the word obey from the ceremony. The word had actually been removed back in 1928, but some people still liked to include it in the ceremony. However, Derek and I were in agreement that neither one of us would 'obey' the other, rather we should communicate with one another, and hopefully always make the right decisions.

At the end of the service, the Reverend Griffin, Derek and I, my chief bridesmaid, and Pat, Derek's best man, retired to the vestry in order to sign the necessary paperwork. After that, we returned to the church, and walked back up the aisle towards the church door, this time as man and wife.

This time I could see faces, so many faces! All my relations were there, my aunts and uncles, my cousins, some of them with their own children. What surprised me, actually astounded me, was the number of my friends who had turned up at the church.

Once outside the church, the photographers took over, and quite some time was spent taking photographs in various parts of the church grounds.

The time came for us to leave the church, and that's when the chaos started. Everybody seemed to have confetti, and Derek and I were almost crushed by those who wanted to shower us with it.

Eventually, we escaped to the safety of the taxi that was to take us to the reception. I remember wishing at that time all those dear friends who had taken the trouble to turn up at the church could have been included in the reception. But we had no way of affording that.

42

The taxi whisked us off again, not very far, possibly half a mile to the place at the bottom of Northgate, where we were to hold our reception. It was a Saturday afternoon in the middle of August, a very busy time in the town centre. I remember the taxi pulling up outside Grainger's Café, and I remember wondering how we were going to manage to cut across the flow of people walking in both directions as they shopped on a Saturday afternoon.

I need not have worried. The taxi driver came round and held open the door for us whilst Derek and I tried to get me and my dress safely out of the taxi and onto the pavement. Having succeeded in actually exiting the taxi, we stood there for a second, Derek clutching the yards of material in my wedding dress, and amazingly there was suddenly a path to the café.

People had actually stopped to let us cross and they clapped and wished us well as we made our way across the very wide pavement.

Once inside, Derek and I were able to look around and appreciate the trouble that Grainger's Café had gone to in order to make this a very special day. Across the side of the room, next to the windows, was the top table and branching out from that were three long tables. The tables were decorated beautifully and the wedding cake took pride of place in the corner of the room. I still remember the smell from the beautiful flowers which had been provided by Graingers.

The rest of the guests arrived a few at a time and Derek and I greeted each and every one. Eventually, when all were present, we sat down for the meal. I know it's becoming harder, actually harder each day, to remember events exactly as they happened and try as I might, I cannot remember the food that was served that day, I just know everybody enjoyed it. Grainger's Café kept up the usual high standards.

There were speeches, people were happy, they laughed a lot and they talked a lot. Everything went well.

I do remember cutting the cake – the most beautiful cake, and I remember being told to keep the small top tier and to use it as a christening cake. However, babies were not on the cards at that time, so I can't remember what happened to it, but I'm sure it was eaten.

The reception came to an end and Derek and I left to go back to Greenbank Road where we changed and picked up our luggage ready for our honeymoon. Times have changed so much since then. The bride and groom in those days were normally packed off quite early to their honeymoon venue, whilst the rest of the wedding guests enjoyed a great party. That is exactly what happened to us.

Back at the house most of the guests at the reception had made their way there, Derek and I were changed and ready to depart for a honeymoon. I changed from my dress into the outfit I had bought specially for honeymoon.

I wore a pale, pink sleeveless dress, with a fitted bodice and flared skirt, which was mid-calf length. There was a delicate floral design etched into the material in black. Over this, I wore a pale pink collarless coat, fitted at the waist, also mid-calf length and slightly flared below the waist. Black court shoes, gloves, and a tiny black hat (more like a headband) with a rose at the side, finished the outfit.

We had booked a hotel in Scarborough and we were travelling to our destination by train. We were taken to the station by taxi, and I remember quite a few taxis accompanied us.

My mum, my Uncle Rob, Derek's mum and Fred and my bridesmaids, best man and groomsmen all came to the station to wave us off. Our train arrived and we got into a compartment. We had corridor trains back then, all with separate compartments, nothing like the open plan with tables that we have nowadays. There were four other people already in our compartment and I'm afraid they were absolutely covered in the confetti that was tossed into that compartment before we were able to leave.

One memory which still sticks in my mind… Derek and I were leaning out of the window to say goodbye. My mother managed to get close to the door and we were about to hug one another to say goodbye when she was literally shoved out of the way by those more determined to be at the front. I know I would have done anything to be able to stop the train so that I could get out and give her a big hug.

43

Those who had gone to the station with us waved goodbye and then returned to 37 Greenbank Road.

My mother had anticipated people staying on at the house and so she had catered for such an event. One of the things she had ordered was ham to make sandwiches. She had asked me to order ham, at the shop just round the corner, which I had done. Imagine her horror when somebody went to pick it up and returned with raw gammon ham. One of the few things she had asked me to do and I had totally messed up. Fortunately, I understand the shop did still have cooked ham so all was resolved. I think the family sorted out the raw ham and shared it out between them to take home to cook at a later date.

Evidently most of the guests ended up staying until late into the evening. Mrs Saint, the taxi driver's wife from next door, came in and played the piano, my piano, non-stop for hours.

No doubt one of my uncles, or my cousins, visited the local off-licence to bring some beers home and my mother possibly had a bottle of sherry ready for the occasion. She was a total non-drinker so alcohol was a thing rarely seen in our house. However, my grandmother loved a glass of milk stout, and enjoyed one every night with her supper, she said the iron it contained was good for her!

Derek and I obviously missed out on the best party that was ever held at 37 Greenbank Road!

We eventually arrived in Scarborough and made our way to the hotel. We were staying at the Boston Hotel high on the cliffs overlooking the North Shore. It was a really nice hotel and we had a lovely room overlooking the sea. Unfortunately any chance we had of arriving 'incognito', in other words trying to pretend we'd been married for years, was doomed to fail from the start. We were covered in confetti; everything we carried was covered in confetti, and they had even managed to get some inside my suitcase. Derek's suitcase, however, was surprisingly free from any sign of confetti. That is because they had picked the wrong case.

Two elderly friends of the family were actually going on holiday straight after my wedding. They had left their suitcases in our house so that they could leave immediately after the reception. Unlucky for them, the culprits who managed to get confetti into my suitcase, picked the wrong suitcase when they thought they had Derek's. This resulted in two very elderly friends of my mother being exceedingly embarrassed when they opened up their suitcase and ended up covering themselves and their bedroom floor in confetti.

But back to Derek and I, and our stay at the Boston Hotel. The room we were given was lovely. The only downside, if there was a downside, was the fact that the door opened into a small porch-like area, part of which was occupied by a large wardrobe. There was just enough room for the door to open fully before it hit the wardrobe.

However, the rest of the room was perfect. Two huge windows looked straight out onto the ocean. Two small, but comfortable, armchairs were situated in front of the windows and made a great place to sit and watch the sea. We looked forward to our stay and the weather up to this point had been perfect and very hot.

The windows in our bedroom were sash windows and the bottom half had been pushed up as far as it would go to let in as much fresh air as possible. The views were much better than anything we had previously experienced. For a while we sat on the chairs provided and just soaked in the view. We decided to skip supper that night as we had eaten our fill at the reception. Also my mother had given us sandwiches and we had wedding cake to eat. Derek went down to the bar and brought a couple of drinks back up and we enjoyed a picnic supper watching the waves breaking on the shore.

There was no such thing as an en-suite room back in the mid-'50s, unless of course you were very rich and I would imagine that very very expensive hotels did have en-suite bedrooms. Most of us had to put up with walking along the corridor to a shared bathroom. It was decided I would use the bathroom first, whilst Derek unpacked his suitcase.

When I returned to the bedroom I was wearing a dressing gown. Thinking that I heard somebody coming along the corridor, I opened our bedroom door quickly, intending to get in there as fast as possible before anybody saw me. Unfortunately, I opened the door just as Derek was placing his empty suitcase on top of the wardrobe. The result was the door hit him hard on the back of his head, and propelled him face first into the wardrobe!

I suppose you can guess what happened next… it was funny to me… funny enough to end up with me in a heap on the bed giggling uncontrollably.

I did manage to control myself temporarily as I examined the back of his head and his face to see if I had caused any real damage, but all looked well. There were no obvious cuts or swellings. However, controlling myself was temporary because as soon as he said he didn't know whether to hold the back of his head or his face, I set off again.

Derek did not say another word. He picked up his toilet bag, his toothbrush and his towel, and left to go to the bathroom. I eventually managed to compose myself, and I unpacked my suitcase.

Whilst Derek was in the bathroom, and I was unpacking my suitcase, the weather outside began to change. The temperature dropped, and a slight breeze developed. When Derek came back to the bedroom, we thought it might be a good idea to close the windows. However, this proved impossible. Whoever had opened them had made sure they would never close again. They were stuck. Totally and completely stuck. Eventually we decided to just leave them as they were. There seemed to be an adequate supply of blankets on the bed and in one of the drawers there were spares in case we became cold in the night!

However, in the middle of the night, we were woken abruptly. It seemed at the time as though there was somebody in the room who was trying to rip the sheets and blankets off the bed. In fact, the top blanket actually took off and ended up on the other side of the room. We shot out of bed and for a moment we were nonplussed as to what to do. It was a bit like being in the middle of a dream. Anything and everything that was lightweight and not fixed to the floor or the wall was flying around the room.

It seemed hurricane-strength winds had developed and were coming straight off the sea. The only thing to do was to have another go at the windows, which by this time were rattling in their frames. It seems the wind had loosened them slightly and this time with effort we did manage to close them.

The next morning we slept later than intended, and when we entered the dining room for breakfast, all eyes turned to look at us. Quite a few reasons. One: I think everybody knew we were newly-weds. Two: we were late for breakfast, in fact they had almost finished serving. Three: we obviously made a lot of noise in the night fighting with the windows, and at that time, nobody knew it was the windows we were fighting with… they just heard a lot of banging!

The Boston Hotel was incredible value for money. It included a fantastic cooked breakfast, coffee and biscuits at 11am, cooked lunch at one, afternoon tea between 4pm and 5pm and what was then called an evening meal or high tea or supper (these days, it would be dinner), was served between 6pm and 7pm. Also, if you were still hungry, coffee, tea and snacks were served between 9pm and 10pm! Whatever the time of day, if you felt hungry or thirsty, your needs were dealt with.

I don't think I have ever stayed at a hotel anywhere since then where I had such value for money, or indeed, so much food!

When I was young we had four meals a day. Breakfast, dinner, which is what we called the meal we had at midday, tea and supper. As we moved around the country, over a period of time, without us even realising it, our vocabulary changed, and we adopted the terminology of the part of the country we lived in.

I now eat lunch at lunchtime, I eat dinner in the early evening and anything eaten late evening is still supper. Other words changed too. The sitting room became the lounge. The scullery became the kitchen. The lavatory became the toilet.

But back to our honeymoon. The first couple of days we spent exploring the area. The weather was good, the food was good, and we had no more trouble with the windows!

Then we met the rest of the young people in the hotel. It was probably the third morning of our stay, and Derek had already gone down to breakfast in order to make sure they knew we were coming, because once again we had overslept. I was racing down the stairs when I collided with a young man who was racing back up the stairs to collect something he had forgotten from his bedroom. It turned out that he was on holiday with his girlfriend, his best mate and his girlfriend. They were our age, and they came from Manchester!

That was actually the beginning of a friendship. Most of the rest of the week was spent in their company, playing cricket on the beach, boating in Peasholm Park, exploring the town. In fact anything and everything that people do on holiday. We were joined by another young couple, I think they came from Lincolnshire.

I remember the eight of us enjoyed a week, full of fun and adventure. We spent most of our time together including mealtimes in the hotel.

Eventually, however, the honeymoon came to an end and it was time to board a train to go home.

44

This time, home for me was in a different place. I was going to live in Cheadle Hulme near Stockport.

I had applied to Manchester Education Authority for a teaching post, and I had been successful in my application. As was the case in Darlington, you were employed by the authority and allocated a school by them. At that time, I had no idea which school I would be working in.

Where we were going to live had been the subject of much discussion. We intended to find somewhere to rent, at least to start with. Auntie Flo had even offered to let us live in her house. However, Derek's mother had other ideas. She insisted that, until we managed to find somewhere else, we lived with her.

Therefore, it was with a mixture of feelings that I boarded the train to Manchester and waved goodbye to Scarborough. I was happy and excited because I was with the person I loved – we had such plans! But I was curious to know what my new school would be like.

Also I was apprehensive. Apprehensive because I was unsure what life would be like living with somebody who had already made it clear to me that she was not at all happy with Derek getting married.

But whatever my feelings, as the train sped through the countryside, each mile that we covered was taking me closer and closer to my new home. To my new life.

We were fortunate enough to have the compartment to ourselves for most of the journey, and we sat opposite one another by the window in order to take in the beauty of the countryside through which we passed.

Sometimes our view was blurred by the steam which passed the window and I remember reciting Robert Louis Stevenson's poem, *"Faster than fairies, faster than witches. Bridges and houses, hedges and ditches,"* in time to the clickety-clack of the wheels on the rails. Once again, I was experiencing the first day of the rest of my life.

A new place to live, a new job, and possibly most important of all a new name. I was no longer Audrey Smith, I was now Audrey Clegg.

And now there were two of us, Mr and Mrs Derek Clegg!

Milton Keynes UK
Ingram Content Group UK Ltd.
UKHW050207230824
447187UK00015B/170

9 781805 144953